Values in World Religions

Lester Mondale is now Leader of the Philadelphia Ethical Society. He received an S.T.B. degree from the Harvard Divinity School in 1929, and has held Unitarian pastorates in Hingham, Massachusetts; Evanston, Illinois; and Kansas City, Missouri.

He has written articles for the *Unitarian Register,* the *Christian Leader,* the *New Humanist,* the *Journal of Liberal Religion,* and the *Ethical Outlook.* Mr. Mondale is also the author of two booklets (*The Missouri Still Runs Wild* and *Three Unitarian Philosophies of Religion*) as well as the book *The Unitarian Way of Life,* which was published by the Beacon Press.

Values in World Religions

Lester Mondale

Starr King Press

Boston

Table of Contents

Preface

Catholic sees Protestantism as a Catholic. Protestant sees Catholicism as a Protestant. Each sees the other's shortcomings with amazing clarity. And with equally amazing blindness each misses the moving spirit, the lift of the other's faith. Jews, similarly, see Christianity as Jews; Christians see Buddhism, Islam, Paganism as Christians. Again, the same awareness of defects; the same blindness to the spirit and power of the other fellow's faith. It has been only in recent years that men have begun to face reality in religion — tried to see other religions for what they actually are, through the eyes not of the missionary or polemicist but of the anthropoligist and scholar. With the assistance of this more scientific-minded seeing one can find in other religions strength for trouble, insights into the ingredients of a more satisfying life, a vision of the broader and deeper significance of this life in this world. The times demand this new kind of appreciation — which is to say, global spirituality. They demand that we go beyond mere tolerance and actively seek in the faiths the fonts of inspiration that have enabled the generations of their devotees to face up to life.

Such is the concern of the following chapters. They are not written as a would-be scholar's treatise or an anthropological dissertation. The purpose is not to cover each religion with encyclopedic wholeness but rather to write to the needs of the layman. His needs, as is brought out in the concluding chapter, call for a distinctive approach to the religions of the world. This approach is not particularly new. One finds approximations in all religions: Zen Buddhist manuals that simplify or popularize the faith for the layman; Vedantist demarcation of higher (that of the religious professional, of course!) and lower Vedanta. This division holds in Catholic Christianity between the faith as it is held and practiced by the theologian and "religious" and the folk faith of the peasantry. If there is anything new and different in the approach of this book it lies in the acceptance of the needs of the layman (as against those of the professional who would find in religion the personality integration that comes of his making religion a full-time vocation)

as the specifications for a re-formation of present-day religious outlook
and practice. The thought is that religion for the new age of plenty
must take its cues from the problems and the hopes and the aspirations
of those who find the better part of their personality integration in
the normal course of living, doing the everyday work of the world. Presented here is but the veriest suggestion of such an approach. If these
several sallies into the treasure house of the world's religions tempt the
reader to investigate further and to search out the additional riches that
are to be had in plenty, this writing will more than have fulfilled its
purpose.

Acknowledgments

Grateful acknowledgment is made to the following for permission to publish excerpts: Mrs. James B. Pratt for quotations from *The Pilgrimage of Buddhism;* Mrs. Paul Hutchinson for quotations from Mr. Hutchinson's article in *Life* (December 26, 1955); the Yivo Institute for Jewish Research, literary executors of the Zhitlowsky estate, for quotations from Chaim Zhitlowsky; Shocken Books, Inc., New York, for a quotation from Martin Buber's *Israel and the World;* Penguin Books Ltd., for a quotation from *Buddhism* (a Pelican book), by Christian Humphreys; Random House for quotations from Lin Yutang's *The Wisdom of Confucius* (copyright 1938 by Random House), and his *The Wisdom of China and India* (copyright 1942 by Random House); Charles Scribner's Sons for quotations from *The Sacred Books by the East* by Max F. Mueller and from *Treasure House of the Living Religions* by Robert E. Hume; George Allen & Unwin, Ltd., for quotations from the *Analects of Confucius,* by Arthur Waley; *The American Scholar* for a quotation from an article by Joseph Wood Krutch, in the Autumn, 1956, issue; E. P. Dutton Company for a quotation from *The Face of Silence,* by Dhan Gopal Mukerji; George G. Harrap, Ltd., London, for the quotation from Owen Ritter's *Triumphant Pilgrimage and English Muslim's Journey;* The Christophers, Ltd., London, for quotations from Ameer Ali's *Spirit of Islam;* The John Day Company for quotations from Lin Yutang's *Importance of Living* (copyright 1937 by The John Day Company, Inc.); the New American Library of World Literature, Inc., the publisher of *The Way of Life* (Lao Tzu), a new translation by R. B. Blakney of *Tao Te Ching* (copyright 1955 by Raymond B. Blakney); Dr. Suzuki and John F. Rider, Publisher, Inc., for quotations from *Zen Buddhism: Selected Writings of Suzuki,* edited by William Barrett; the Philosophical Library, Inc., for quotations from Suzuki's *An Introduction to Zen Buddhism;* The Macmillan Company for quotations from Willard Sperry's *Reality in Worship* (copyright 1925 by The Macmillan Company); the Harvill Press, Ltd., London, and Sharon Books, New York, for quotations from Joseph

Baratz's *A Village by the Jordan;* Beacon Press and Columbia University Press for a quotation from Gilbert Murray's *Five Stages of Greek Religion;* Mr. Leonard Sussman, Executive Director of the American Council for Judaism, for the prefatory note to the chapter on Judaism.

I have been unsuccessful in locating the book or periodical in which "Rhyme of the Times" appeared; I trust that a promise of due acknowledgment in forthcoming editions will suffice.

I wish to acknowledge with thanks the invaluable assistance given by the staff of the Philadelphia Public Library in looking up publishers and addresses and assisting in the double checking of more than one hard-to-come-by oriental translation and quotation. Finally, to Charlotte Robinson, my painstaking secretary, who has borne the brunt of typing, retyping, tedious letter transcribing, and communicating with the Philadelphia Public Library, my heartiest thanks.

Religious institutions and procedures which are supposed to be objective expressions of the reality of faith are so often and in so many different ways contrary to true faith and to the truth of faith. They have become stumbling blocks in the path of the true believer; they have placed themselves in opposition to his humble life, and on the side of whatever happens to be powerful and accepted as valid in this world. This error, which is in the foreground of our time, has affected the souls of the generations which grew up in a time of crisis; it has invalidated their faith. Here again, the right has been abandoned along with the wrong. Real faith does not mean professing what we hold true in a ready-made formula. On the contrary: it means holding ourselves open to the unconditional mystery which we encounter in every sphere of our life and which cannot be comprised in any formula. It means that, from the very roots of our being, we should always be prepared to live with this mystery as one being lives with another. Real faith means the ability to endure life in the face of this mystery. The forms in which the mystery approaches us are nothing but our personal experiences. At times it is very difficult to live with the mystery and to be constant to it in the midst of these ever new, unforseen, surprising, precipitating and overpowering experiences. But there is something which can help us and there are helpers. There is the living transmission of those who have really lived with the mystery, and above all those who are of our kind and who had our tidings.

Martin Buber, *Israel and the World*

We spent the better part of a week in this great monastery [T'an Che Ssu, near Peking], visiting by day its temples and shrines, talking with its monks, attending its religious services, and tramping over the hills that surround it, by night sleeping in one of its courts or wandering through its spacious ways, bathed in moonlight, the like of which, as I believe, has never been elsewhere on land or sea. In a Buddhist temple such as this, one seems transported to another world. The spaciousness of the place with its innumerable buildings ranged in charming disorder up and down a hillside, its gleaming roofs of green and yellow tiles and swaying contours, looking over each other's shoulders from the varied levels of the slope, the stone-paved courts with their great trees and little flowers and alluring vistas, the palatial stairways with their elaborately carved marble railings, the little shrines at unexpected intervals and the solemn temples in whose darkened recesses sit the Buddhas on their lotus thrones. . . . In such a setting the chanting of Buddha's praises by the monks seems something eternally appropriate. Long before dawn it begins and this early service is followed by others at occasional intervals through the day, the last coming at the end of the evening. About nine o'clock — soon after moonrise — one of the smaller gongs is heard from a little shrine opening on the principal court. This is answered by the deep notes of the great gong at the entrance. Then a wooden gong from another place joins the chorus and the silvery treble of a little bell from a new direction. The gray figure of a monk now appears, crossing the lower court in the moonlight and climbing the broad marble staircase before the temple; others silently follow, coming from different parts of the great monastery, one by one, swimming through the luminous darkness. One of them opens the temple doors, lights the candles on the altar and the incense sticks. The other monks steal in after him through the moonbeams and the shadows. *They bow and prostrate themselves before the Buddha and the chanting begins.*

I like to think that it continues: that at every dawn and every evening the things of the spirit are not forgotten; that there are many places, even in practical China, where the smoke of incense and the praises of the Blessed One are still streaming upward, through sunrise and cloud shadow and moonlight, as they do at T'an Che Ssu.

J. B. Pratt, *The Pilgrimage of Buddhism*

The Consolations of Buddhism

Buddhism, an expert on the subject has written, is not *a* religion. It is a *"family* of religions." So much of a family is it that anything one might say about any member of that family could be contradicted by some world traveler who is acquainted only with another member of that amazing family of religions. If, for instance, one were to say that Buddhism has been the great civilizer of the Orient, the teacher these 2,500 years of gentleness, tenderness, love in all human relations, this could be flatly denied by someone who may have had to flee for his life from excited Buddhist lamas of Tibet, or who knows the part Buddhism played for centuries in Japan in the development of the art of self-defense, Judo, and how it has been used there to reinforce the morale of the soldiers and officers. Both persons could be quite correct. One might spend hours describing the intricacies of the philosophy, the metaphysics, that monks are supposed to master. One could go on to quote a succession of passages such as this, from a contemporary Buddhist explaining Buddhist philosophy:

> *"Be-ness" is the highest which man can conceive of the Absolute. It manifests on a universal playground of space-time called the Dharma-Dhatu, and all within this field of Samsara partakes of the essential nature of Be-ness, which is called, for want of another name, Tathata, "Suchness." To coalesce one's personal consciousness with the indwelling essence of Suchness is Nirvana.*[1]

Everything one might lay before readers about the intricacies and subtleties of Buddhist philosophy can be truthfully contradicted by the traveler who knows only of those millions who believe that they need do no more to win Nirvana in the end than repeat hundreds of times a day: "Namu Amida Butsu." If one says that the Buddhist believes in no soul and cherishes no future life, someone else can insist

---

[1] Christmas Humphreys, *Buddhism* (Penguin Books Ltd.), p. 148.

1

with equal truth that the Buddhist is as much worried about getting into the heaven that many of them call the "Pure Land" as the orthodox Christian is in getting into the heaven of the pearly gates. One might assert that Buddhism is quite at home in the new world of science and psychology. Another could rightfully contradict the assertion with the observation that magic and sorcery and superstition are of the very essence of Buddhism. One might say that in no religion in the world is there to be found such unbounded compassion or love for all living things, including the animals and the plants. This could be countered with the well-taken protest: "In no religion in the world is there to be found selfishness to compare with the selfish self-centeredness of Buddhist monks." One monk was heard to say:

> *You have mother and father and sisters? Leave all to themselves and think only of yourself, pay no attention to them. If you get rid of lust, anger, and ignorance you will have happy life. To love your husband or your father is very dangerous. If you live pure life without attachments you will be young and good-looking when you will attain eighty or hundred years. If I live good life I will be young and well with no infirmities when I get old.*[2]

One can state truthfully that genuine Buddhism, the old original Theravada or Hinayana Buddhism, is simple and Protestant-like. But another who has traveled extensively in China, Tibet, Korea, Japan, can protest: "Protestant? Whoever could call temple services with the sounding of gongs, and burning of incense and candles, and bowing before images and chanting hymns and prayers in a language foreign to the worshipers, and the counting of beads, all in all a Mass-like service, Protestant!" He is talking about the Mahayana or Catholic branch of the family — also quite legitimate.

What is Nirvana? Complete detachment from all creation and from self? A higher attachment in the form of an overflowing love and concern for all mankind? A trance experience? A blissful realization that comes only with death? A mystical vision? The answer depends wholly on the particular Buddhist to whom one may be talking, or the Pali text one is reading.

[2] J. B. Pratt, *Pilgrimage of Buddhism* (Macmillan Co.), p. 137.

It is regrettable, perhaps, that one should have to bewilder the inquiring reader with these many complexities. But the fact is that if he weren't left bewildered he'd have no real sense of the luxuriance and richness and inclusiveness of this great family of religions with its 250,000,000 — or is it 500,000,000? —followers. One finds both figures.

To the structure of Buddhist complexity and bewilderment we have been building we must now add a completing dome. If one were to say, which is true, that Buddhism, with its emphasis on each person's being an island to himself, a refuge to himself alone, is highly humanistic, another person, whose travels may have acquainted him with Buddhism in the lands to the north of India, could retort with righteous indignation: "Humanistic? Ridiculous! How can you call humanistic the ornate temples with their dozens, yes, their hundreds of gods — call the gods Buddhas and Bodhisattvas, but gods nevertheless — with priests and laymen bowing down before those images and directing their prayers to them?" Again, both would be correct. The family as a whole is both humanistic and theistic. The paradoxical truth of Buddhist worship or devotion came out in the answer a Burmese monk made to a British bishop who had curtly demanded to know: "To whom are you praying and for what?" The pious monk replied with equal curtness: "I am praying to nobody for nothing."

Paradox, complexity, contradiction — thy name is Budhism! But for all of this confusion there runs throughout the entire family a certain indefinable resemblance, a unity that makes the family very definitely a family. The likeness is the unity, among other things, of the image that is sculptured and painted and engraved in every temple, pagoda and corner-cupboard home shrine throughout the whole vast extent of the world of Buddhadom: Siddhartha Gotama, sitting cross-legged among the petals of a huge lotus blossom, eyes closed in bliss, a faint smile on his lips. This is the image of Siddhartha in the moment of his becoming the enlightened one, the Buddha.

Connected inseparably with this image is the old, old story of the fabulously pampered young Prince Siddhartha of the Sakya clan: fluttering droves of servants to serve his slightest wish; palaces for each season of the year; every meal a banquet; entertainment to suit any whim and fancy; concubines galore — all the satisfactions here on earth that the poor and downtrodden of the ages have looked forward to enjoying only in some heaven in the hereafter. But this heaven on earth the young prince renounced, and with it he renounced the wife and infant son he loved, and he took to the woods. There he joined the company of aristocrat beggars, men who like himself had been hounded by the conviction that man has need of something more satisfying; that he is cut out for a destiny more important than basking life away in gardens of luxury. Then came fruitless years of cultivating trance states — and then more fruitless years of mortifying the flesh, even to the point of death. Finally under the Bodhi tree, the great enlightenment and the bliss of the inner peace that came with the enlightenment. All this is everywhere suggested by the image of the Buddha: the epitome of serenity and inner triumph over circumstances, to which so many millions daily bow their heads and direct their meditations. Enshrined in heart and mind the image helps them through the turmoil and jostlings and disappointments of the hours ahead.

It is not mere happenstance that Buddhist monasteries (and there are thousands of them in Asia) are located wherever possible in beautiful mountain clefts or near small lakes where the lotus can grow and the birds and the fish live undisturbed. "There," relates a traveler, "I have paddled among thousands of blue-winged teal — usually very unapproachable — gathered in the heat of the day, to sleep and preen their plumage, and have all but stroked them with a paddle." They know that near the monastery they will be unharmed. In wandering through a monastic establishment this same traveler noticed on a high shelf a small, exquisitely carved figure of the Buddha. He turned to the abbot who was with him and requested that the carving be taken down so that he could examine it. The monk's hand went up to the shelf, and as he grasped the statuette red ants swarmed over his hand and arm and peppered the skin with pimply spots. "The abbot," said the traveler, "did not change his expression or quicken his movements in the least but put the figure down and placed the ants on a neighboring shrub."

Looking at the central figure and symbol of this great family of religions we ask the question that is to be at the forefront in this book: "What is there for us in all this?" If the serene person who is portrayed in this statue or image were by some miracle able to speak to us, his answering words, strangely and paradoxically, would not be words of bliss and serenity. They would express the insight that came to Siddhartha under the Bodhi tree: that all existence is suffering, that to live, to exist, is to suffer. "Birth is suffering; decay is suffering; illness is suffering; death is suffering. Presence of objects we hate is suffering; separation from objects we love is suffering; not to obtain what we desire is suffering. Clinging to existence is suffering."

Everybody suffering? Twenty-five hundred years ago, possibly. But today? With all the promise of the oncoming electronic revolution? With thinking machines already here that can remember 100,000,000 facts, read and write electronically at the rate of 2,000 words per second? Suffering when we'll soon have mechanical devices to do all our remembering and thinking for us? Typewriters in the immediate offing that can transpose the dictated word directly into the written word; windows with automatic eyes that will open or close them as the weather changes; color television with flat screens hung beside oil paintings on the living-room wall? For the suffering of a cold, an antibiotic. For an ache or pain, any one of the new miracle pain-relievers appearing on the market each week. For injured feelings, a new hat, a new car, a trip around the world. Everything available in increasing abundance for the alleviation of every symptom of suffering. So what is suffering to the modern mind but a sickly illusion, a consequence of negative thinking? If you are a sufferer with crosses to bear, then you must be unhealthy or abnormal. So don't ever for one minute give yourself away. Smile. Put on the smile one sees on the lips of every happy cigarette smoker and whiskey drinker and clothes horse and new-car owner in the magazine advertisements — and of every politician up to and including the President, and even the Vice-President! This is the age of the smile.

But behind the rosy appearance and gladsome front, what? It seems that the husband and wife you meet are so happy, so nicely mated: that you and your wife must be the exceptions with your problems; your periodic falling out of love; your despair, at times, of inspiring each other; your failings with your children. But never think it. Those who may seem the most successful, counselors tell us, are not strangers to domestic trouble and suffering, but those who have accepted the fact of ever-recurring differences and difficulties and who keep persistently at it to make of their problems something more than frigidity and broken homes. The other fellow seems so talented, so brilliant, and you, with your lack of talent or gifts or even aptitude — what can be your lot but the shallows and miseries of mediocrity? Here is another of the false notions exposed by psychological therapeutics: it is the talented one who suffers — frustrated for lack of energy and time to make the most of what he has, bogged down in indecision as to which of his talents to develop.

You would live in peace and good will with your fellows. But along with this good resolution you had better brace yourself for the suffering of the slurs, the machinations, the knifing and trouble-making of the ever-present neurotic whose personality integration is the negative integration of fear and ill will and hate; who as a consequence is forever bent on stirring up trouble in which he can make himself a center of attention, and in which he can also fulfill his frustrated need for belonging by way of the seeming nearness, the pseudo-friendship, of those who for the fleeting moment happen to be on his side. You would have everyone meet as friends, as brothers, with no exclusion, no segregation anywhere. You do your best to break down the barriers that artificially separate man from man. But will you ever be rid of the unrelenting pain of feeling left out: the Jew left out of certain inner circles of Judaism; the Negro left out of the various inner circles of the colored; the Catholic left out of the select circle around the bishop; Protestant Nazarene or Pentecostal Disciple ill at ease among Presbyterians and Episcopalians?

Someone asks: "How are you?" You don't answer that you are suffering. What you say in answer is a casual, "Oh, I'm all right." All the while the undertone of the answer, the intimation between the words, is: "I may be a little on edge, or a little under the weather, or a bit worried, tired, at the moment." Ask yourself how you really feel in this present moment, and how often you do find yourself suffering. But then the brave smile and the assurance: "But tomorrow when I've had a chance to rest, next week, when I get this big job out of the way, then I'll be myself again. When I get this puzzling office snarl untangled, then . . . when I get over this cold . . . when I get the children through school . . . when I get in my Social Security time . . . when I write my book . . . when I retire . . ." All of which is to say: "When I'm dead . . ." In the present moment there is always some kind of suffering, and seldom if ever is there any grappling with the fact that suffering is forever causing us to postpone, postpone and postpone the hour when we are really going to begin to *live*.

Suffering is still real and suffering is still universal, and there is no getting away from the fact — not in the paradises of India's rajas and maharajas, or even in electronic utopias! This situation raises the question: "If we can't get away from suffering, what can we do about it?" The root cause of all our sufferings, the Enlightened One taught, was what might be called desire or thirst or craving. Only by overcoming or eradicating craving or desire can we do away with suffering. It is the image of one who has overcome or mastered desire that we see in the Buddha in the lotus.

We look to that image again and we wonder how the Buddha's message may be of help to us. Overcoming suffering by overcoming or eradicating desire? "Wait a minute," we protest. "What is it but desire for food, for friends, for home, for husband, for wife, for the welfare of our children, for making something of ourselves, for life itself, that integrates the personality and makes living worth the while? Without desire what is one but a corpse?"

True enough. But that, we are told on good authority, wasn't exactly what the Buddha meant. The condition of which he was speaking is with us still today, and in monstrously exaggerated proportions: cravings, thirsts, desires whipped up to roaring forest-fire proportions by every conceivable device of science and art. Craving not only for finer clothes and finer homes and finer friends and finer wines but also craving for recognition, for books the making of which there is still no end, for legitimate stage performances, and music, and art exhibits, and meetings and meetings and meetings. The times are an unholy conspiracy to transform desire, craving, thirst into the gargantuan appetite that will engorge the ever-increasing production of the goods and services of this age of plenty. The trend, if we were simply to give way to it, would make us into frenzied monsters of consumption.

Often the only thing that can bring us back to something like our human and normal selves is a jolt: the surgery or the heart condition that has us convalescing flat on the back and out of the race for weeks; the round of duty as the army draftee; the death or divorce that opens our eyes to the all-importance of some of the simpler, quieter satisfactions and moments we have been overlooking in the universal rat-race of climbing and consuming. What is this breather, this moment of sanity that comes with the jolt, but an overcoming, for the moment at least, of the frenzies and the sufferings of desire?

In renouncing his princely paradise, Siddhartha Gotama refused to become a monster of appetite. That was one side of his overcoming of desire. The other side of his way to the mastery of desire is illustrated by his turning away from the five ascetics who had taught him that to deal with craving one must starve it out, kill it off. Under their direction he had starved the flesh to the point that his eyes bulged from their sockets, his ribs stuck out, and he looked like a mummy. But for all this mortification of the flesh, he had no relief from suffering. He could go no farther, and he knew it. He took some rice and sour milk. Then, as the scriptural account has it, "having taken solid food and gained strength . . . I attained and abode in joy and pleasure."

To handle desire, he found, you don't root it out; you don't let yourself become a monster of appetite. You give to the flesh such food as it legitimately demands. By so doing you put an end to what can be a degradingly obsessive desire. How degrading the desire for bread alone can be was brought home to me by a man who went through starvation for months, in Germany after the conclusion of the First World War. "The thought of food," he said, "connected itself with everything that came into my head. I felt like an animal."

As it is with the desires of the flesh, so is it with all other desires. Take desire for recognition, which is a legitimate human need: the desire for recognition is not to be mastered by starving it to death with humility, and it is not to be satiated by promotions and newspaper write-ups and elections to office and community prominence. Both the lack of recognition and the gluttonous pursuit of notoriety spell suffering. What is the desire for recognition, in essence, but a phase of man's larger desire for acceptance, for belonging? And for this the only food that alleviates and gives freedom from desire is the warmth, the affection, the appreciation that comes to one in response to his own outgoing warmth and affection and appreciation.

Minister to the flesh as did the Buddha. Minister to the need for belonging, as the Buddha did so beautifully and with such unceasing compassion during the forty-five years of his wanderings. And then, because the ministry must be to the desires of the whole man, one will find himself going on in some way to parallel the Buddha's famous eight-fold path: to the handling of the desires of the mind with *right belief;* to the handling of the desire to achieve and create with *right aspiration;* the desire to communicate with people with *right speech;* on to *right behavior; right livelihood; right effort; right mindfulness;*

right concentration. Give to each level of the desires of the whole man its appropriate gratification, and then in the reasonably healthy mind and body no one of the desires will get out of hand and become obsessive or compulsive and a cause of anxiety and hence of suffering.

It isn't hard to see why so many millions look with reverence and devotion to the figure of the serene Buddha on the lotus blossom. The image bespeaks the satisfactions of that day of enlightenment under the Bodhi tree, the cravings of his flesh for the first time in years assuaged, his mind no longer focused hypnotically on the pains with which he had been struggling, and magnifying in the struggle. At ease in repose his was the satisfaction, the joy, that all of restless mankind was so frenziedly pursuing; what those who starved their bodies were after; what the rajas hoped to find in their futile and sensual amusements; what the struggling and sweating masses imagined would be theirs if only they possessed the wealth and the prominence of the rajas. His was the state of mind that is open and responsive to the glory of the surrounding infinitudes of mystery as well as to the miracle and wonder of selfhood. Thus to all who are harried and heavy laden by the desires evoked in us and in our children and in the Joneses by the vast machinery of advertising and promotion, the image of the Buddha in the lotus blossom looms up with ever-greater magnitude and significance and beauty.

But suppose our suffering is from desire that is of a different order of attachment. Suppose it is the suffering of inconsolable grief, the pain of a loneliness for a departed one whose death has left an emptiness so vast that it is inconceivable that anyone else can fill it. Here, again, the central image of Buddhism does not fail the anguished spirit of man. For all of its twenty-five centuries it has been the consolation of sorrow and grief — not with the promise of better things in some future life to come, but in and with the spirit of Siddhartha Gotama himself. His answer to the ultimate in grief was that of the young mother I knew many years ago. This mother was a beautiful woman, but a semi-invalid and confined to a wheel chair. In a dream she saw her six-year-old son and her ten-year-old daughter at her funeral; she saw them in the mourners' pew, unkempt, untidy, forlorn. The dream had considerable reality to it because she did have an incurable ailment, and she knew that her days were few. On awakening, her answer to that dream was not moaning and sobbing and making everyone miserable, but wheeling her invalid's chair to the telephone and ordering from the local stores many samples of cloth. Then she bought yards and yards. Throughout the succeeding days, as long as her strength held up, the household heard the clicking, the whirring of the electric sewing machine turning out sun suits, play suits, sports dresses, house dresses, school dresses, party dresses. And what a radiance of satisfaction and peace was on the face of that good woman when I called on her and she had the dresser drawers opened and I saw drawer on drawer of tidy new garments; for the summer she never lived to see, for the winter — literally for years ahead.

In the words of the ancient Buddhist hymn (Sutta-Nipata) : "As a mother, heedless of danger, stands between harm and her little one, her only child, let men, in their minds, embrace all living things. Let this embrace, unblemished by hate or ill well, include all the world, withholding naught."

The central symbol of Buddhism is not, as so often has been said by the misinformed, the picture of world-negating escapism, of unheroic surrender to evil, of unmanly and unwomanly quietism. The peace of the Buddha is like nothing so much as the peace of the giant generators of the power houses at the foot of Niagara Falls. There I have stood and listened. I heard almost no sound — nothing, certainly, in comparison to the noise kicked up by a little one-lung gasoline washing machine or lawnmower engine. And yet there was being generated and silently put out on wires the power of more than a hundred thousand little one-lungers. The Buddha image is the Niagara dynamo, the inner life not dead or quiescent, but very much alive; all parts moving in unison — quietly, peacefully generating the power that the historic Buddha manifested with such epoch-making results when he turned his compassion on his suffering fellows, so desperately in need of the attuning and the adjusting he himself had found in that historic moment of illumination under the Bodhi tree.

The Enduring Humanism of Confucius

About thirty-five years ago there began to appear in liberal pulpits and on college faculties of this country men who called themselves Humanists — John Dietrich, Curtis Reese, Eustace Haydon, Max Otto, Roy Wood Sellars, John Dewey. These men were Humanists, they insisted, not theists. Their loyalty was to man, and not to the God of Christianity or Judaism. Their concern was with this life and with the natural, not with some future life and the supernatural. Their authority was science and philosophy and human experience, and not some book of revelation. In these thirty-five years Humanists have been called everything from atheists and free lovers to communists. It is the Humanist that the orthodox Christian and Jew have in mind in particular when they shout denunciations of that horrendous threat to democracy and religion and home and family they call *secularism*. It is the alleged decadence of Humanism from which Congress and the President have been trying to protect us, by way of legislation that puts God on postage stamps and into the oath of allegiance. Humanism, theologians confidently assure us, is a superficial rationalism, a philosophy that stands up only as long as the weather is fair and the sailing is smooth — nothing for a blizzard or years of drought or hurricane devastations.

No one could have been more the humanist than Confucius — respecter of the religious beliefs of other men, respecter also of the *way* of heaven — but at the same time one who, when asked about the worship of celestial and earthly spirits and about death, had to answer in all honesty: "We don't know yet how to serve men; how can we know about serving the spirits? We don't know yet about life; how can we know about death?"[1] First for him was man and first among his concerns for man was this life. For 2,500 years, some hundred generations, this humanism has ministered to the daily needs of countless Chinese in fair weather and foul.

[1] Lin Yutang, *The Wisdom of Confucius* (Random House), p. 184.

In writing of the humanism of Confucius I do so fully aware of the shortcomings of Confucianism. Chief among the shortcomings is the filial piety of which Confucius made so much, and which in his day was well and good. His esteem for the family was illustrated in the answer he made to a duke who had boasted that among his people were men so upright that if a father were to steal a sheep his son would testify against him. Confucius replied: "Among us the upright act quite differently. The son shields his father, and the father shields his son; we see this as uprightness." This principle of familial loyalty is illustrated in the sacrifices of the Chinese peasant family to enable one of its brighter sons to go on to school and thus to secure a governmental position — and then, with that son in office, in his being loyal before all else, including public welfare, to his brothers and his sisters and brothers-in-law, to his cousins and his uncles and his aunts. This principle is probably China's greatest political weakness, the source of the infamous "Chinese squeeze." Because of the squeeze only a small portion of shiploads of food sent by Americans to famine-stricken areas in the interior of China ever reached the starving. Along the way each petty official had to extract his family "take" regardless. The squeeze, extended to all governmental offices and to all governmental functions, made for the universal corruption that left China the helpless prey of imperialist European nations, Japan, and finally, of Communism.

Confucius didn't get along with women, and one is not surprised. His own wife apparently left him. His daughter-in-law divorced his son. His granddaughter-in-law divorced his grandson! For all of that his direct descendants make up a considerable clan in present-day China. Confucius — literally, Master Kung — demanded bedclothes half again the normal length, to keep his feet warm. He was an unusually tall man. His coats had to have the right sleeve tailored shorter than the left, for convenience at his writing. His mat had to be laid out properly or he wouldn't sit on it. His meat had to be cut into fine pieces, be fresh and served with the right sauce, or he wouldn't eat it. He wouldn't eat, either, unless there was ginger on the table. He hated the new music of his time. What he said about it gives expression to feelings of many a present-day parent whose teen-age children are worshipers of the renditions of the current Adonis of the "cool cats":

Now in this new music, people bend their bodies while they move back and forth, there is a deluge of immoral sounds without form or restraint, and the actors . . . mix with the company of men and women, behaving as if they didn't know who were their parents or children.[2]

For all of his quaint peculiarities and tastes Confucius was a man who could weep for his friend, smile and laugh and really care for people. About himself he said:

I am a man who pursues the truth untiringly, and teaches people unceasingly, and who forgets to eat when he is enthusiastic about something, and forgets all his worries when he is happy or elated, and who is not aware that old age is coming on. . . .[3]

The most serious, also the most common, criticism of Confucius — that he was an arch-conservative worshiper of the idealized empires and emperors of the past — is in reality no criticism at all. The truth, as the painstaking scholar H. G. Creel of the University of Chicago has been bringing out in recent years, is that Confucius, far from being an arch-conservative, was in reality an arch-revolutionary. If he revered China's mythical golden age it was because in its rulers and legendary kings he found standards of personal righteousness and of conduct of public affairs that he and all future generations could, and actually did, hold above the behavior of any present king or emperor. The same holds true of the Analects — his sayings, collected by his scholar-disciples. These have been learned and treasured by all succeeding generations. Their sum total effect has been to make the Chinese individualistic in their thinking, for no teacher in all times has been more the encourager of each person's thinking for himself. Thanks to the Analects the Chinese are generally liberal-minded in intellectual outlook, pacifistic or at least unmilitaristic in temperament, and, hence, people that are hardly likely to be moulded in any great hurry into orthodox, Marxian, goose-stepping fanatics and militarists. The Titoist rumblings in China today, suggesting a growing independence of Moscow, are but a natural consequence of all these generations of devotion to the sayings of the great Master of China.

[2] L. Yutang, *op. cit.,* p. 263.
[3] *Ibid.,* p. 79.

Perhaps a word about the Analects is in order before we go on to more specific questions as to what Confucius has for us. The Analects that most of us have read in the past, and probably found not too inspiring, were translations of well-meaning but religiously near-sighted scholars. If these translators (as anyone can see for himself if he will compare their translations with the more sensitive renderings by Arthur Waley) had rendered the twenty-third Psalm as they have the Analects, the Psalm would not read: "The Lord is my shepherd. I shall not want. He maketh me to lie down in green pastures; he leadeth me beside still waters." Instead it would read: "My god is a sheep herder. I am one of his sheep. I am not afraid that there won't be enough for me to eat. I can rely on him to drive me to fields where I will have green grass to eat. There I will have a hole with plenty of water in it." The Analects, as Lin Yutang so rightly insists, are not to be read in one sitting, but one saying at a time, while the reader ponders the meaning, possibly for hours, until its larger and deeper significance dawns upon him. They are that rich in insight.

The times to which Confucius addressed his life are so markedly similar to the world of today that the needs to which he ministered 2,500 years ago are also very much the needs of the present hour. If, by some miracle of supernatural religion or clever device of science fiction, old Kung-fu-tze could be resurrected and could scan the headlines we have been reading in recent years, he would shake his head and smile and comment: "How familiar!" He'd feel quite at home amid the international anarchy and the struggle-to-exist turmoil of today! Treaties are still observed as they were in his time when, as one ruler frankly put it, a compact was something one lived up to until circumstances gave him the advantage over the other fellow. His was a world dominated by military force. One survived by an all's-fair-in-war cunning, corruption and brutality. A king who was a near contemporary of Confucius, a local Hitler or Stalin or Franco, receiving bad news from a messenger, pulled his sword and cut the throats of the seven men who happened to be in his tent at the time. Thus did he censor the news. Hired murderers, torture and mutilation were as common then as they have come to be again in our own age. Parents and children, brothers, sisters, like members of families in totalitarian states, could no longer trust each other.

These tactics have been taken over by the communists and made the working principles of their revolution. This means that on every front where communists are at work (and on what front are they or their sympathizers not at work?) any means whatsoever — deceit, secretiveness, boring-from-within, encouragement of factionalism — that will give them power, goes. This holds true in the most insignificant local welfare committee or liberal or labor group as well as in the government itself. Any grudge, any discontent, any hurt feeling is never too petty to encourage if it will make for dissension and for more of a following for the agitators. More than once have I seen Communists who deny with righteous indignation any connection with the Communist party, or with Moscow at least, profess their undying liberalism, their devotion to American democracy, and then in the same breath go on to accuse some genuine liberal, who happened to differ on a point of fact or principle, of being the liar, the conspirator, the reactionary social fascist, the enemy of progress. The end result of all this is the breakdown of the values that make for decent living together, communication, truth-telling, fair play, good will; the breakdown, finally, of the feeling of belonging. The contentious individual stands at last an isolated, unloving and unlovable atom of self, alone under the glittering stars of infinitude.

The social consequences of moral breakdown were vividly dramatized, when Confucius was about thirty years old, in the case of the ruler of the kingdom of Wu. An ambitious relative invited him to a banquet with the idea of murdering him and taking over his domains. The ruler of Wu suspected foul play. Nevertheless, he accepted. He came, incidentally, with troops of soldiers who lined the road from the palace to the entertainment hall of his gracious host. In the banquet hall the guest posted his armed guards. These met every waiter bringing food, stripped him on the spot, made him change clothes, and then compelled him to crawl in on his hands and knees, accompanied by two men with drawn swords. One would think that these rather pointed precautions ought to have been enough to convince the host that his guest and relative was suspicious and on his guard! But the cunning plotter was not to be outdone. He had a servant conceal in a baked fish a dagger which, as the fish was set before the king, the servant seized and then employed with lethal consequences.

In the midst of that sinister dog-eat-dog social chaos and indignity there arose a prophet, a scholar-teacher-prophet, one Confucius, who addressed himself to the dukes and kings. This prophet spoke with the voice and conviction of one who himself had known the privations of the exploited and the pillaged. To the head of one kingdom and then of another he said, in effect: "You can no longer trust either your higher or your lower officials, not your brothers, or your sons, not even your own mothers. Such is the sad and sordid pass to which you have come! But here, here in me, is someone you can trust, someone who can put your kingdom in order, and in putting it in order make its people happy and loyal and the country strong. Try me. I'm a different kind of career person. I'm not the cunning conspirator who will outsmart everyone who is plotting against you, not the master deceiver, not the clever liar and schemer who will hoodwink the masses of your people. For all of my book learning I'm really a very simple and direct kind of person. I'm one who believes that first in all our relations with each other there must be simple honesty and truth."

The most powerful man in Confucius' home kingdom of Lu was an autocrat by the name of Chi K'ang. This man, as H. G. Creel has pointed out, would have had as "much compunction about having Confucius tortured to death as about crushing a fly." But when Chi asked Confucius' advice on how he might deal more effectively with thieves the scholar-prophet replied: "If you, sir, did not covet things that don't belong to you, they wouldn't steal if you paid them to!" Chi waged predatory wars; he lived in ostentatious luxury; he gouged his people with taxes. He had everyone afraid and in awe of him — everyone but Confucius, who "in almost every statement [about Chi K'ang] that has come down to us, is outspokenly critical," which is to say, truthful and trustworthy.

Confucius' desire to place simple honesty and truth first in all relations with his fellow men came out of his discovery of a new and more satisfying relationship between men; a quality of living that was infinitely more satisfying than dealing with people only for what one can get out of them, for what power or advantage one can get over them, for what prestige or sensual gratification they might afford one.

We come upon this more satisfying relationship in the account of his striking out (when he was fifty years old — his hope for service in his home kingdom of Lu abandoned) in search of a neighboring king or duke who might take him on as chief minister of state. More than one of Confucius' followers had been employed in government. As the decades went on more and more of these trustworthy men were taken on — until China became blessed with a new peace and order. But for Confucius, on the verge of becoming an old man, his was a hopeless mission. Year followed year of fruitless wanderings and dangerous encounters. With him was always a goodly handful of his student-disciples, sons of aristocracy, sons of peasants with only dried meat to pay for their instruction. He took them all, the only provision being that they had to be able to think for themselves and be dedicated to the cause of a better lot for their fellow men. The relationships he struck up with these followers and in whatever village or city or court he visited was expressed by a symbol he had painted on a shingle and placed on his tent. It was the symbol for the word "Shu." This word or character means: "My heart's desire is to meet your heart's desire," or, "My heart responds to yours." Not do unto others as you would have them do unto you, but *feel* towards others as you would have them *feel* towards you.

The depth of the meaning of this attitude was brought home to me when making a call on an elderly Jew in Kansas City. He was the founder and owner of a large and thriving furniture store. But he was old and down with a heart condition. As a boy this man had seen the massacring of friends and relatives in Russia. But he had never let hate, he said, become a part of him. A statement he made that afternoon might as well have come from the lips of Confucius. He said: "He whose heart is in the smallest degree set on goodness will dislike no one." This was the opposite of the old idea in our culture, that one can be as sweet as sugar on the surface and yet within be hating the person one is dealing with, and "get by" with it. The truth is, as this store owner so nicely illustrated it, we don't "get by" with it. He told of a man who started out in business next door to him. But he failed. Why? The Jew told him why. He said: "When a Jew comes into your store you can't be cordial to him, because in your heart you don't feel cordial and he senses it. And so with a Negro, and so with labor union men, and with anyone who doesn't belong to your political party — bitterness and more bitterness. Your trouble is that there are so many toward whom you feel unkindly that there aren't enough left to keep you in business!"

It is this right feeling, this right mental attitude toward others, that was stressed by Confucius:

There are three things that a gentleman . . . places above all the rest: from every attitude and every gesture that he employs he must remove all trace of violence or arrogance; every look he composes in his face must betoken good faith; from every word he utters, from every intonation, he must remove all trace of coarseness or impropriety.[4]

Among the prophets of the world's religions is no one who ministers with more healing effect to that shivering and helpless isolation, to that loss of feeling of belonging, to that state of lovelessness that comes of the breakdown of truth and honesty and fair play and good will in man's dealings with man.

But this isn't the only condition to which this scholar-prophet of ancient China still speaks with eloquence and healing. He speaks to those of us who have been caught, who have been made tense and anxious and heavy laden by the burden described by Joseph Wood Krutch. Krutch sees all of us — scholar and worker, gentleman and businessman — entangled and degraded by all that is suggested in the slogan of the airlines: "Have fun now; pay later." In the same vein we hear: "Spend all you earn. Go into debt. Buy on credit. Get a new car just as soon as there is a change in style of the chrome trimming. Do your loyal part in keeping the national surpluses down. Keep the men in the automobile factories at their jobs. Discard everything which is still as good as ever." Prosperity depends not on living within our incomes but in everyone's exceeding them. Poor Richard must now read: "Waste or you will want." "The surest way of bringing a rainy day is to prepare for it." Concludes Krutch:

At various times, various cultures have assigned their own characteristic reasons for believing in the sacredness of human life and in the value of each individual man. Once it was that every man had an immortal soul. In less religious but romantic ages it was usually that he had a unique personality. Then in societies dominated by utilitarian thought, it became that he could produce something. But now, at last, it is only that he can use something up. Scorn not the Common Man, says the Age of Abundance.

[4] Arthur Waley, *Analects of Confucius* (George Allen & Unwin, Ltd.), Book VIII, p. 133.

He may have no soul; his personality may be exactly the same as his neighbor's; and he may not produce anything worth having. But, thank God, he consumes. . . . He performs his essential function, and we honor him for it.[5]

Today, as seldom before, we need the example of someone, of some group, that stands out and away from all the frantic millions of the other-directed consumer crowd, and exemplifies a new kind of dignity. It is to this need that Confucius comes with his concept of the gentleman, the superior man. He demonstrated the role of the superior man once when, on his travels in search of a royal patron, he and his followers were surrounded in the countryside by soldiers of an unfriendly prince. There was no slipping away, no procuring of supplies. The blockade went on day after day. Food ran low. Several in the party became ill and were confined to bed. Unable to do anything about the situation, Confucius spent his time reading and singing and accompanying himself with a string instrument. Irritated at the seeming ineffectuality of his Master, one Tselu came to Confucius and asked ironically: "Does a gentleman sometimes also find himself in adversity?"

"Yes," answered old Kung, "a gentleman also sometimes finds himself in adversity, but when a common man finds himself in adversity, he forgets himself and does all sorts of foolish things."

The superior man is superior to adversity. And if I find myself in want, with "coarse food to eat, water to drink, and my bended arm for a pillow," then, added Confucius, "I still have joy in the midst of these things. . . . The cultivator of the soil may have his fill of good things, but the cultivator of the mind will enjoy a continual feast."

While still surrounded by soldiers the Master called his leading disciples in one at a time to ask if they thought his teachings were wrong. "How is it that I find myself in this situation?" he asked. The third to be questioned answered him: "The Master's teachings are so great. That is why the world cannot accept them. However, you should just do your best to spread the ideas. What do you care if they are not accepted? If the truth is not cultivated, the shame is ours. What do you care if you are not accepted?" Smilingly Confucius turned on him

[5] Joseph Wood Krutch, "If You Don't Mind My Saying So . . ." *American Scholar*, Autumn, 1956.

and said: "Oh, son of Yen, if you were a rich man I would be your butler!"

If the truth is not cultivated, the shame is ours; for who but we are the ones who benefit the most? If you are not accepted what do you care; for aren't you accepted in the company of these scholar-gentlemen? Accompanying these satisfactions, this kind of success and distinction, are those equally delightful satisfactions of the heart suggested by the picture of Confucius singing and playing.

One summery day, when the times were better for the Master and his followers, he was seated with four students. Confucius turned to each of them and asked what he would do if he were free to do exactly what he liked. The first, self-confident and ambitious, answered that he'd like most of all to be given the governorship of a weak state to show what a strong utopia he could make of it in three years. The second, somewhat less self-confident and ambitious, answered that he also would like to be a governor, but that his interest was to make it possible for everyone in the nation to have enough to eat, then to see what the effect would be on the people. The third, a retiring soul, answered that he'd love to shut himself in the state temple and there spend his life studying the ancient rituals. Confucius then turned to the fourth, named Tien, who up to that moment had been strumming his lute and humming softly. He laid the instrument aside, and rose to his feet as if unwilling to answer. "My ambitions," he said, "are altogether different from theirs."

"Never mind," said the Master. "Tell us what they are."

"Well, it is near the end of spring. What I should like to do would be to change into light clothes, join a little company of youths, go with them to bathe in the river, enjoy the breeze and dance among the wood-shrines, and come home singing."

"Ah Tien," sighed Confucius, "I feel just like you."

In the concept of the Confucian gentleman, of the superior man, the ancient Chinese were given a new hope for a better kind of government and new goals in living. Confronted with the glowering face of a petty autocrat, with the mealy-mouthed flattery of the Machiavellian politico, with rags and poverty, with over-seriousness, or the involvements of wealth, the one who aspired to a better kind of life had but to remind himself: "I am a Confucian. I am a gentleman." And merely in the thought, in the concept of what he was, he saw differently, he felt differently, he acted differently — exactly as does the young man today when he can say to himself for the first time: "I am a doctor," "I am a lawyer," "I am a scientist"; or the young woman, "I am an artist," "I am a teacher," "I am a mother." Reminding himself: "I am a Confucian gentleman," he could stand, as did a disciple admired by Confucius, in a tattered hemp-quilted gown — stand beside others wearing costly furs, "without the slightest embarrassment."

The Confucian gentleman had about him something that was vastly more dignifying than costly furs. He had what Confucius referred to as "Li" — politeness, decorum, social grace. He stood out in contrast to the rude, with whom Confucius said nothing could be done, the rotten wood that is not fit for carving:

> *A man who is impulsive and headstrong without hav-
> ing the virtue of simple honesty, who doesn't know a thing
> and has not enough wit to speak or behave cautiously, or
> who has no particular ability and withal has not the virtue
> of honesty or faithfulness....*[6]

The gentleman, as H. G. Creel has pointed out, was like the justices of the United States Supreme Court, who start each day by shaking hands with one another before walking into court. Justice Byrnes thought this custom was somewhat inane until he learned how, many years before, a chief justice had established the custom "on the theory that no matter how heated the arguments of the justices might have been the previous day, they would be able to reconcile their differences if they started the day with a handshake and on speaking terms."

Here in the image of the gentleman-scholar-humanitarian was a new and satisfying way. It led throughout life from height to height, with something most worth while — fellowship of richest fare, feasts of the mind and heart — to look forward to always.

Said Confucius:
> *At fifteen I set my heart upon learning.*
> *At thirty, I had planted my feet firm upon the ground.*
> *At forty, I no longer suffered from perplexities.*
> *At fifty, I knew what were the biddings of Heaven.*
> *At sixty, I heard them with docile ear.*

[6] L. Yutang, *op. cit.*, p. 197.

*At seventy, I could follow the dictates of my own heart;
for what I desired no longer overstepped the bound-
aries of right.*[7]

In other words, at seventy, when he could follow the dictates of
his heart — at seventy rather than at forty — is when life can still begin!

---

[7] Legge, trans., *Analects* (Charles Scribner's Sons), Book II.

Vedanta: The Religion of Finding the Self

At the Parliament of Religions, held during the Chicago World's Fair in 1893, one of the delegates from India, Swami Vivekananda, rose to speak before an audience of some seven thousand persons. He uttered but five words: "Sisters and Brothers of America . . ." So moving was the emotional quality of those five words, as well as the effect of the Swami's colorful garb and presence, that it brought the audience spontaneously to its feet for several minutes of uninterrupted cheering and applauding. Vivekananda became the sensation of the Parliament. He was regularly listed as the last speaker on any program. In that way they made sure that audiences would remain to the end. He was athletic, handsome, well-read in Western science and philosophy. The lecture tour that followed was little short of a continental triumphal procession. To the busybody West he preached peace and quiet and meditation — and mysticism. It was in this way that America was first introduced to Vedanta, by a missionary for whom it was a philosophy of everyday living. Vivekananda was followed by other swamis who set up Vedanta centers in New York, Boston, Chicago, Los Angeles; by 1945, thirteen in all. Among those attracted to their ranks are Christopher Isherwood, Gerald Heard and Aldous Huxley.

Swami Vivekananda came to America as the disciple of a Hindu saint, Sri Ramakrishna. It is said that on one of Vivekananda's first visits to the old man — he was then a law student — they sat on the ground facing each other, looking in silence; the man of spirit confronting the youth of the comely flesh. Then without a word the holy one lifted his right foot and shoved it toward the young man until it touched his body. "That instant," Vivekananda is supposed to have testified later on, "before my wide-open eyes the walls of the room reeled and fell; then the furniture, possessed by some demoniac force, dashed itself on the floor, then sank into a void. All around me was Nothing, Nothing!" Terrified at the thought that this void of nothingness was about to swallow and annihilate him, the words flashed into his mind: "Oh! You! What are you doing to me? I want to live. Do not let me die yet . . ." Then, with a touch to the chest, and consoling words from the holy man, the furniture and room rearranged themselves — leaving a bewildered and not a little shaken young student.[1]

Here was a strange person, a strange power and realm of experience that invited investigation. The investigation led to Vivekananda's becoming a disciple.

Ramakrishna as a youth had been the adoring priest of the goddess Kali. Later he had accepted, legally, the girl who, according to custom, had been selected for his wife. He placed her in separate quarters; for what was the physical body, as one of his American followers has written, but a "bag of filth?" His sole concern was for the spirit, for what to him was the true Self and at the same time the indwelling God. Giving way, letting go completely and absolutely to this higher something within, which he regarded as the indwelling Atman or Brahma or God, he became, seemingly, god-possessed. God-possessed he was buoyantly happy — so much so that he gave everyone the impression that he was always "at a party that never stopped." On every person and everything he looked with eyes of love. Despite this saintliness he was not above singing or getting to his feet and dancing if musicians wandered by, or even clowning to amuse young boys. In the full ecstasy of god-possession, which could come upon him at any time or place without warning, he became so absorbed, so lost in the trance, that he dropped in a heap. To protect him from falling and dislocating his bones, which he did on one occasion, disciples had to be constantly at his side wherever he went.

It is this joy, this happiness, this bliss of the god-possession, god-consciousness, of Ramakrishna that the modern Vedanta swamis and their distinguished laymen followers hold up as the one goal that can give life meaning and worth commensurate with its true dignity. It is our one sure salvation, supposedly, from the anxiety, the "nerves," of the doggerel by Virginia Braiser entitled "Rhyme of the Times":

> *This is the age*
> *Of the half-read page*
> *And the quick hash*
> *And the mad dash.*
> *The bright night*
> *With the nerves tight.*

[1] Dhan Gopal Mukerjii, *The Face of Silence* (E. P. Dutton), pp. 115-116.

The plane hop
And the brief stop.
The lamp tan
In a short span.
The big shot
In a good spot.
And the brain strain
And the heart pain
And the cat naps
Till the spring snaps
And the fun's done.

If what has been laid before the reader by way of introduction to the religion or philosophy of Vedanta has aroused anything comparable to the interest that was quickened in young Vivekananda and, latterly, in such persons as Gerald Heard and Aldous Huxley, then he will want to go on to investigate these things. We will evaluate them, of course, from our own more naturalistic, practical point of view — trying all things and holding fast to that which is good.

It is my conviction, let it be said at the outset, that Vedanta has something of inestimable value for those of us who are so much the sad victims of the half-read page and the quick hash and the mad dash. But it is also my conviction that one does not get the best of Vedanta in the highly theistic and mystical form in which it has been presented to the West by the Swami Vivekananda and laymen followers of Ramakrishna. I see no supreme good, no supreme goal, not even pleasant diversion in the bliss and ecstasy of god-realization, the unceasing spiritual party of Ramakrishna. What is more, I can imagine no world more dismal and uninviting than one in which the bulk of humanity had been won over to the celibate Ramakrishna as the ideal man; in which they spent the better part of their time in spiritual exercises; and in which they had to rely on the remainder of humanity to be present always at their sides to see that in their unpredictable trancelike seizures they didn't fall against furniture and granite curbs, into oncoming traffic, out of open windows, or down river banks!

The Vedanta philosophy or religion goes back more than 2,000 years beyond Ramakrishna. It goes back to a time in ancient India when middle-aged men were leaving their jobs and their homes in numbers, as did the Buddha, and going to the forests. In doing this they had the daring to put into practice and to act upon that which such a large proportion of men in our own time and our own culture only dreams of doing. They made the break from the half-read page to the quietly and carefully read great book; from the quick hash to the savored and appreciated morsel; from the mad dash to the unhurried listening of the ears to the patter of the rain or the wind soughing through the trees, to the unhurried opening of the eyes to the shining sublimity of the galaxies overhead.

Acting on the dream of getting away to something less harrowing and more satisfying was, as those early Hindu philosophers saw it, only in the natural course of living. To them any man's life was to be thought of as divided into four stages or epochs of growth. First in the natural order of things came the student period, the learning years. Then, secondly, came the householder period — marriage, babies, child-rearing, providing. It is here, with these two alone, where we of the West customarily stop. In middle age we merely go on being the householder provider; making of life a game of acquiring the most imposing of houses, the most sumptuous of provisions. And this continues year on end, and without end until the breathing of the last labored breath. This painful process is pointedly described in the recent book, *The Executive Life,* by the editor of *Fortune.* A reviewer in *The Reporter* describes how executives sweat in order to become higher executives — their "riding of the whirligig"; and then, when the aspirant has "come into his kingdom" among the top executives, the "promotion neurosis . . . generally characterized by a great anxiety, psychosomatic symptoms and emotional conflict . . . . While outwardly playing the part of a corporate Man of Distinction and regularly addressing Chambers of Commerce luncheons on the splendors of the American Way, he is inwardly haunted by doubt and obsessions of inadequacy."

It is here that the ancient Hindu philosopher comes up with the idea of two more stages of growth. As he saw it, the developing and unfolding life of man comes naturally to a third stage where "the man in the grey flannel suit," instead of obliterating all doubts in a frenzy of work, takes time out to do some meditative evaluating: "This vice-presidency, along with 146 other vice-presidents in the Bank of America, 119 others in the Chase Manhattan — is it worth ulcers or a heart attack? That magnificent salary raise, of which I will get only eight percent after the Federal tax collectors have helped themselves! A secretarial assistant officially labeled a *stenographer* if I am a junior executive; a *secretary* for me if I am an executive; a *senior secretary* if I make a vice-presidency. I wonder." There comes for everyone, women as well as men, a time for a radical facing of facts, an agonizing reappraisal and transvaluation. These fleeting hours and days and years; are they to be no more than a half-conscious delirium of whirl? Or can one emulate Adlai Stevenson, who, after the conclusion of his 1956 campaign, said that the time had come for him "to forsake the hot debate and go out under the stars and listen" for a while.

When one has come to this point in his development he can begin to appreciate the significance of the discovery that is at the heart of Vedanta. This discovery, let me say in anticipation, prepares one for the fourth stage of life; a period that comes voluntarily or involuntarily to all if we but live long enough. It is the period of walking alone, which can be a time of desperate and ghastly loneliness, or, if properly prepared for, a time of freedom and serenity, of feeling that "the whole world is one's home, all living beings one's kith and kin."

What the forest philosophers discovered is described in those ancient speculative writings known as the Upanishads; and the essence of the Upanishads is to be found in the poetic work, often referred to as the New Testament of Hindu scriptures, the Bhagavad Gita. According to these writings the satisfying life that everyone is after exists in no hereafter and in no heaven of ease and luxury and security that one can create for himself in the here and the now. All too long had the Upanishad philosophers watched the masses of the people offering their sacrifices, pouring out their prayers and libations to Indra, Varuna, Mitra, Agni, and for all their devotions receiving in return no more rain and no more-plentiful crops, and no relief from the exactions of their oppressors. Their devotions altered not a whit the course of nature. Nature's behavior, they were coming to understand, was essentially an order, not the caprice of the gods. Turning from the disappointments of this life to the promise of the next, the masses began to devote their sacrifices to making sure that the good things they cherished would be their lot in the hereafter; as if the ease and luxury and security of some mansion in heaven would be any more satisfying to the spirit than was Siddhartha Gotama's princely heaven on earth!

Heaven, with the peace of mind or whatever it is everyone is after, is tied up, the Upanishad philosophers insisted, with the discovery and the finding of the self. An intimation of what is meant by the discovery or finding of self appeared in the recent newspaper story of the fifty-year-old Wisconsin shoe-factory employee who had been all but blind since his sixth year. On this man's one eye surgeons performed a corneal transplantation; then sent him home with a bandage over the eye. Three weeks later the bandage was removed. The patient wrote his surgeon:

> *That night my wife took the bandages off. It took about an hour before I was able to keep the eye open. When the eye finally stayed open, I was in the kitchen. It was wonderful to see marble design on the floor. I looked at the cabinets. I never knew that wood could be so pretty. By this time the tears were flowing. Our family was together and it seemed like Christmas Eve to me.*
>
> *After that I made a slow tour through the whole house looking over every nook and corner. The colors and the painting were so wonderful. I just am not able to explain how good it felt to be able to see. I told my wife that I hated to go to bed that night for fear that I would wake and that it was a dream.*

The following morning he insisted that his wife remain in bed while he got up and made the breakfast:

> *"I put the eggs in the pan. What a sight to see the beautiful color the yolks were. It made me wonder how you could get hungry when you can't see how good the food looks to you!"*

To one person that kitchen was but another kitchen. But to this man with an eye that was really seeing, it was a dream world. All of which goes to prove that the supreme good, the heaven that all men are after, is to be found, as the Hindu philosophers discovered, in themselves. Which is also to say that the supreme bad, the hell on earth from which most men are so madly fleeing, is also to be found in themselves.

From all this it was only logical that the philosophers should go on to further explorations in the self. What they found is suggested in the setting of the Bhagavad Gita itself. The scene is a battlefield on the eve of battle. The central character is Arjuna, commander of the Pandavas. He is a member of the warrior caste, a warrior by profession. The Gita is one long conversation between Arjuna and Krishna, the god incarnate in Arjuna's charioteer. It was probably the religious revolt of Arjuna's warrior caste against the priestly Brahmin caste with their endless sacrificing to the gods, that resulted in the self philosophy expressed in the Upanishads and later in the Bhagavad Gita. That the philosophy had its origin in the warrior caste is probable because there is no one for whom self-possession is so all important as it is to the warrior. We see this exemplified in the eminent French field marshal, Viscount Turenne. As he was about to leave his quarters to plunge into the thick of a crucial battle he was seized with a violent fit of trembling. This was in the presence of his officers. The trembling was nature taking over with one of its most ancient protective devices. Next in order was the wild beating of the heart, the dryness of the throat, the panting breath; then the panic that reduces thinking power to zero and makes a blank of the mind. Nature was incapacitating him for anything but running for his life or dropping in a heap in a convenient hideaway. Worse still for Turenne was the morale-destroying effect of such a spectacle on his officers, for nothing is as contagious as fear. Instead of letting nature take over completely he emphasized that in himself was that which sets man apart from the instinctive biological mechanism, the mere beast. He got hold of himself, as we express it. He looked on at his trembling hands and knees and said aloud before the officers: "Tremble body. You would tremble yet more if you knew that into which I am now going to take you."

Turenne had a self. In essence he was a self that could detach itself from the trembling of hands and knees; that could refuse to be panicked; that could stand apart. Once that self is possessed and is standing apart in a moment of trouble and anxiety and danger, then, it goes without saying, one begins to recover strength and competence.

It is this self-possession that is at the heart of all courage. The self of the heroic one refuses to become entangled in the anticipated sufferings, the debilitating fears and anxieties that have the coward dying so many times before his death. The possessed self looks on with composure at the prospect of whatever may lie in the offing — wounds,

suffering, death itself. If he is the genuine warrior he is also, paradoxically — and this is true to history — the happy warrior. Not overly
attached to life he is in a position to savor his life adventurously, to
the last enjoyable morsel of its potentialities.

All this has its applications in daily living. In Chicago I used to
hear it said of this man or that on LaSalle Street (the street where the
money used to be made in Chicago) that he would never get rich.
Why? "He loves money too much." Lacking was the detachment,
the courage, in other words, to make the most of the game that the
big operator on LaSalle Street was supposed to make of it in those days.
In the same way we can love our children too much, our jobs too much,
our friends too much; become so self-entangled that it is beneficial
neither for ourselves nor for others. In sickness and pain it is the person who lets physical discomfort and distress *get* him, get his *self*, who
suffers most wretchedly and who is the dreariest burden on others. But
if one can detach the self from one's miseries and see in them something amusing (as did Irving Cobb, who complained, with mock bitterness to the nurse taking his temperature, over the almost total inadequacy of the nourishment he was able to extract from her thermometer)
how differently one feels, how vastly easier it is on others!

The extent to which self can stand apart and transcend pain and
suffering is illustrated by the Vedanta saint Ramakrishna. In 1885
he suffered a severe hemorrhage of the throat. Physicians diagnosed
cancer. He lived on for almost a year. Despite his suffering and the
pain of using any of the muscles in the throat region, he continued as
usual to instruct his disciples, to joke, to laugh, to sing — as if the
party of life had not been interfered with in the least. He looked on
his body wasting away "with a kind of calm, secret amusement, as
though this horrible disease were only a masquerade." So thoroughgoing was his nonattachment that he had some of his following doubt-
ing if he suffered at all!

The effects of self-possession are as powerful on others as they are
on one's own person. The moving power of one who is well on the
way to the finding of self appears in the contrast between one of Thomas
Hart Benton's World War II pictures and the Russian word picture
of the martyred death of their partisan Zoya.

On Benton's canvas are three sub-human monsters, representing
the Axis powers, thrusting a massive spear into the side of a man bound

to a cross. At him from a swastika-marked warplane overhead is directed a fiery stream of lead. His body is writhing. His chest bulges. His shoulders are thrown back. His face is turned upward. His opened mouth has the shape of screaming agony. In this figure one sees no self or evidence of selfhood; only the frenzied agony of the terrified and tortured animal. It is a pathetic scene that makes one cringe at the bestial horror of it all. In this picture Benton unfortunately did his deserved reputation for breadth of conception a grave injustice.

In the Russian word picture, put together out of newspaper clippings at the time, the eighteen-year-old Zoya, member of a guerrilla band, has been captured. She has been tortured for information. Blood, according to the Russian account, seeps from a wound in her forehead and from her fingers and from her feet as the captors lead her to the gallows. But not one word of information have they been able to wring from her. On the platform, as they are about to drop the noose over her head, she calls out, not like Benton's screaming figure, but as a human being who has a self that can disentangle itself from pain and from fear and horror and regard even death with contempt. She calls to the watching Russian villagers, "Comrades! Don't look so despondent! I am not afraid to die. They will hang me, but I am not alone. There are two hundred million of us. Victory will be ours! Goodbye, comrades. Don't be afraid. Stalin is with us. Stalin will come!" With her death and the published story of her death an electric thrill flashed through the nations of Russia. That young girl's heroism and courage, her noble self-detachment, lifted millions of Russians above the animal fear of death and drove them with doubled and tripled determination into the gigantic counter-attacking push that carried them to the very banks of the Rhine.

Explorations into the nature and potentialities of self have uncovered so many insights that are of consequence to all, and the explorations go out in so many directions, that the best one can do in the space of a chapter is to give but the veriest hint of what lies beyond. With each step toward self-discovery the self becomes more amazing and at the same time more wrapped in mystery.

As has been suggested, the one who is self-possessed in the hour of suffering or enfeeblement or danger is ennobling and inspirational. But the self that is not merely *got hold of* but that is *given,* given by the mother to her child, given by the speaker to his listeners, by the musician to his audience, by the singer pouring her very soul bird-like into her song — what is more satisfying to others? This brings to mind a remark made some years ago about a young minister who had failed to make the grade. A parishioner commented on how informative his sermons were, how hard he worked. "But he could never quite give us himself." Without that giving of the self — giving of the self also by one marriage partner to the other, to children, to friends, to the person one happens to meet in the most casual of business relationships — without the greatest of gifts we are poor indeed. Our relationships are nothing and we are nothing.

Beyond getting hold of self and beyond giving of self is that even more breath-taking power of the self to identify itself with others. This was the message of a father to his young daughter who for the first time had come upon the realization of death as something that applied to her. She was about eleven. To her father she said: "I don't want to die ever. I just can't bear the thought of it, not to be able to see or to play or be with friends or do anything. It almost makes me afraid." To the child the father tried to explain first of all how natural and necessary death is; how wretched the world would be if it were filled up only with old people and there were no young people and babies coming on. He continued: "Dying isn't half as sad and half as real as you may think. Of course, if something were to happen to you, if you were to be killed by a speeding automobile or were to be drowned, it would be almost worse than death for me. This is what happens, my child, as one grows older. He finds himself more and more living into, more identified with, the play, the hopes, the plans, the homes of those for whom he has lived so much of his time and his life. And if those who mean so much to him, really more than life itself, go on, and their children in turn go on, what's there about dying to make him afraid?"

In the last weeks of his life Sri Ramakrishna was unable to take food. He was implored by his followers to pray to the Goddess Kali for his recovery; recovery not for his own sake but for theirs. He prayed. She appeared to him in a vision. He often saw visions and this was nothing uncommon. She pointed to his followers asking: "What? Aren't you eating enough through all those mouths?" He reported back to his disciples: "I was ashamed. I couldn't say another word." So extensive are the powers of the self for identification, for empathy, as we tend to put it these days, that getting the ultimate in satisfaction out of eating through the mouths of others, loving through the hearts of others, hoping and planning and dreaming through the minds of others and yet others to come, is not at all farfetched.

One finds himself at last asking in wonderment about the self: "What is this self one must find if he is to be at peace with his mind and with his flesh; this self that can rise above suffering and pain and literally lift the body along with it; this miraculous something that one must find if he is to draw strength and gladness from those with whom he moves from day to day? What is this self that it should move persons to the depths when it goes out to an audience in the nightingale voice of the singer; that it should mean more than all else when it comes to persons in a friendly smile, in a loving embrace?" The classic New World answer comes from Emerson in his essay on the oversoul:

> *What we commonly call man, the eating, drinking, planting, counting man does not, as we know him, represent himself, but misrepresents himself. Him we do not respect, but the soul, whose organ he is, would he let it appear through his action, would make our knees bend. When it breathes through his intellect, it is genius; when it breathes through his will, it is virtue; when it flows through his affection, it is love. And the blindness of the intellect begins, when it would be something of itself. The weakness of the will begins, when the individual would be something of himself. All reform aims, in some one particular, to let the soul have its way through us; in other words, to engage us to obey.*

Now, and finally — to carry Emerson's thought to the conclusion to which the Vedanta philosophers pushed it: is it by any chance possible that the self, the Atman, as they would have it, when fully known turns out to be one with the Atman, or the Brahma essence of the world about us? That is a question that must be left to every person to answer out of the depths of his own personal experience. At any rate it leaves us on the threshhold of the wonderful and the mysterious, if not actually the sublime.

The Reassurances of Islam

That Islam should have anything of spiritual value for Americans of the twentieth century would seem improbable to the point of absurdity to anyone whose knowledge of the faith is limited to what he may have seen or heard or smelled on a tour, in recent years, of the Holy Land, or Egypt, or any other Near Eastern country under Moslem domination. This must have been the feeling of William O. Douglas of the U. S. Supreme Court, struggling to keep a straight face, when he was taken to the Mosque of the Dome of the Rock in Jerusalem. There he was shown the evidence of Islam's claim to Jerusalem as its own Holy City. That mosque was built in 688 A.D. Under the building's huge rotunda his attention was called to the rock, from which Mohammed, he was told, took off on his overnight journey to heaven. As the Prophet ascended the rock tried to take after him. But the angel Gabriel grabbed it and plumped it back into place on earth where it belonged. On the rock are to be seen the distinct outlines of the imprint of the foot of Mohammed. Douglas estimated its shoe size as fifteen or sixteen. Mark Twain in his *Innocents Abroad* put it at eighteen. Also in the rock are the imprints of Gabriel's fingers, of equally gargantuan proportions.

Islam's claim to Jerusalem as its Holy City would seem to be sheer absurdity, as are so many other aspects of its faith and culture: its jihads or holy wars; the medieval or patristic-mindedness of so many of its scholars; its reverence for Mecca and the ritual mummery around and about the Kaaba and the Black Stone; the low estate of the Moslem woman; the almost universally low level of its culture and its economic and political life. All these, together with many another absurdity, tempt the casual traveler and the casual reader to dismiss the whole of Islam with a gesture of contempt.

We go from this to another, and I hope, higher, level of understanding when we group with the Moslem claims, those of the Christian: their holy spots in Palestine, including the sepulcher in which a man who had been dead for three days was supposedly resurrected to life in the flesh, and the mount from which the risen Jesus is supposed to have ascended in the flesh to heaven — both absurdities to the Jew. With these claims we have the long memories of the Jewish stake in Palestine: the Maccabees, Solomon, David, Abraham, as well as the story of the prophet Elijah with his ascension to heaven in a chariot of fire — again in the flesh! Christianity has its absurdities and Judaism also has its absurdities. So, also, does Islam. But for all of that, each in its own way seems to have buried in the verbiage and dogmas and impossibilities of its faith the psychological wherewithal to give to the nobody the feeling that he is still something of a somebody; to the weak and the maimed of spirit the strength to stand up to the strong; to the lost and the bewildered a sense of direction and of mission.

Of all the world's religions Islam is the most difficult for the person of Jewish or Christian background to evaluate objectively. At the present moment any attempt at objectivity is complicated by the prejudices arising out of the conflict between Jew and Egyptian and Arab in general. The temptation is for the Jew unthinkingly to damn Islam as such for what Israel has suffered from the Arabs; for the Arab unthinkingly to damn international Judaism for the military and political setbacks he has suffered from the Israelis. The nationalist Egyptian would like to make of the conflict a holy war that would enlist all of Islam against the Jew. The nationalist Israeli would also make of the conflict another holy war that would enlist all of Judaism and Christianity as well. But to think of these nationalistic tensions as tensions that are essentially religious is not only unfortunate but also dangerous, indescribably dangerous. Israel's battle is not in reality with Islam as such but with national powers: with Egypt, with Syria, with Jordan, with Lebanon (which is fifty-one percent Christian), and, most of all, with the insatiable imperialism of Russia. In this connection one must never let himself forget that standing squarely in the path of Russian advance to the south, effectively blocking her way, are other Moslem nations, important, cherished allies and near-allies: Turkey, Iran, Pakistan, and, farther to the east, Moslem Malaya and Moslem Indonesia.

As far as Israel is concerned with Islam as such, it may well be that her best and long-term hope lies not so much in the crushing and defeat of Islamic power, which could be disastrous for Israel itself, as in the promise of the world-wide renaissance that seems to be under way in Moslem circles. I venture this thought in the full awareness of how little evidence there is to be picked up by the casual observer in the Moslem Near East (even by as seasoned a traveler as Justice Douglas) to the effect that Islam has the capacity for any kind of civilized renaissance. If I am wrong in this, we would still have ample reason for an appreciative study of Islam; for there is no escaping the problem of learning how to live in cooperation with this anything-but-inconsequential one-seventh of the world's population.

That all Islam is quickening with some kind of awakening to self-consciousness and power is self-evident. One thing they are sure of: no longer are these peoples, however backward they may appear to Americans, going to be the willing and wretchedly exploited servants of imperialist Christian nations. That is no longer the will of Allah: not in the Dutch East Indies, now Indonesia, numbering with their Malay brothers some 70,000,000; not in British India, now Pakistan, numbering with their brothers in India, some 100,000,000; not in British Egypt, now simply Egypt, with some 24,000,000; not in Tunisia and Algeria, where France is literally being bled to death; not in French Syria, now simply Syria; not in Iraq, or Transjordan, or Iran. Islam, with some 50,000,000 followers in Africa, is propagating with a vigor that far exceeds that of the Christian population, with its paltry 11,000,000 (including some 3,000,000 Abyssinians whose Christianity is so farfetched as to be Christian in name only). In India and Ceylon the increase has been approximately fifty percent in the last fifty or sixty years.

What is likely to come of this world-wide stirring of new life is anyone's guess. It does mean trouble. But that it might well bring with it a genuine cultural renaissance — with something of value to us as individuals as well as to the world as a whole — is not only my hope but also my personal expectation. Islam, contrary to what most persons have been led to believe, was once the cultural and humanistic light of the world, before the Moors were so ruthlessly crushed and exterminated by barbaric Christians of Spain; and their north African brothers crushed and overrun by the barbaric Berbers; and their eastern brothers crushed and overrun successively by the barbaric and bloodthirsty hordes of Mongols and Tartars and Turks.

The spirit of Islam, the spirit, that is, of Mohammed and of the

Koran, shone forth in its purest light, according to the contemporary and world-renowned Moslem scholar, Ameer Ali, during Europe's Dark Ages. Ali points out that at a time when education for women and property rights for women were almost nonexistent among Christians, when the Jew was being massacred or exiled or at best hounded into ghettos, when heretics and infidels were being burned wholesale at the stake, and pagan tribes were being converted to Christianity at the point of the sword, the Moorish conquerors of Spain wrote into the basic law of the land that Christian and Jew were not only to have security of person and property, not only the right to fill all civil offices and serve in the army if they so desired, but also were to have free use of their places of worship and the free exercise of their religious practices. This toleration of Christian and Jew, far from being an innovation, was merely another instance of universal Islamic practice. To the world Jewry the Moors sent an invitation to come to Spain. There extensive areas had been depopulated by the barbarian invasions. At one time more than 50,000 Jews, men and women and children, migrated to Andalusia, where, under the protecting and friendly arm of the Moslem, they lived in freedom and equality; lived that way for some 600 or 700 years, until that sad and black hour of Spain's reconquest by Ferdinand and Isabella.

With Christian reconquest came the end of universities in general and higher education for women; the end also of the science of astronomy. Having no idea what to do with the observatory tower now known as the Giralda (erected in Seville for the great Arab mathematician and astronomer, Jabir ibn Afiah), they turned it into a belfry! Libraries went up in flames. Astronomers, historians, philosophers, mathematicians, poets, scholars of world renown disappeared or were burned at the stake or made slaves along with countless Moslem women and children. Hospitals and the competent medicine and surgery for which the Moslems were famous became things of the past. Cordova, once celebrated for its cleanliness and beauty, became more like contemporary London with its unrelieved sky line of hovels and "stench in its streets such that no one could breathe its air with impunity."

It is with no little justification that scholar Ali goes on to point out what might have taken place in Europe had the Moors been but a little more on their toes in their battle with Charles Martel at Tours in 732.

With Islam reigning in Europe there would have been no ghettos, no massacres of Jews, Albigenses, Huguenots, or Irish Catholics, no burning of Bruno and Servetus, no Inquisition, no Thirty Years' War of religions. The Renaissance could have been accelerated by some 700 years. Even so, despite the defeat of the Moors by Charles Martel, the better part of mathematics, of philosophy, of scholarship, of astronomy and of medicine that finally did flower into the Renaissance came to Europe initially by way of the Moslems.

All of us have heard of slavery in the Moslem hinterlands, and have heard correctly. But what we have not heard is that Mohammed insisted that the believer who freed his slaves would enjoy great merit in the sight of Allah; that the Moslem slave had and has his legal liberties and his rights, and that he has generally been treated with a consideration that is saintly in contrast to the treatment of the American Negro by his Christian owners in the rice swamps of the South. Most persons have heard of Moslem superstition, of the primitive demonism and exorcism to be found in Islamic countries, of the antics of the pilgrims circling the Kaaba and kissing the Black Stone. They have heard of the outbursts and murderous violence of some of the many fanatical Moslem sects. Again, what has been heard is unfortunately correct. But these aberrations are in fact no more characteristic of Islam at its best than is the unseemly behavior of yowling Holy Rollers or bloody Penitentes characteristic of Christianity at its best; than are Jews at the Wailing Wall in Jerusalem characteristic of Judaism at its best. Mohammed took over from Christianity the idea of a last judgment, of hell. But characteristic of Mohammed and of Islam is the assurance of the Prophet: "A time will come over hell when its gates will clash against each other because there will be no one left in it."

Mohammed himself has been cursed and damned as have few men in history. Dante put him in hell, with his body permanently slit open for his sins of "scandal and schism." Luther calls him "horrid devil." Generally in Christendom he has been known as the "lying prophet," a sensualist, a near-madman epileptic, an ignorant and unlettered plunderer of caravans and cities, a killer. Exactly what to make of the man is a first-rate puzzler. Born into one of the most prominent families of Mecca, and a man of wealth himself, he could not have been anything but a sincere prophet, standing up as he did in the face of years of bitter opposition; insisting that there was but one God, and only one

God, in contrast to the contemporary faith in the many gods and idols of the sacred Kaaba that brought to Mecca swarms of pilgrims who meant much to the city's prosperity. Rich and powerful families became alarmed and hostile. A relative of the Prophet, fearful of an outbreak of violence and striving to appease the hostile, followed him through the streets and after his every utterance shouted, "Impostor!" Children were set to pelting him with refuse and compost. And still he went on reciting, we are told, with never as much as a raised hand to ward off a blow or a missile, never an angry look. He called on his fellow Arabs to give more alms to the poor, to treat their beasts of burden with greater kindness, to cease burying their daughters in the sands, to treat their wives with greater consideration. His uncle, the head of the family, tried to bribe and wheedle him away from his fantastic gospel of monotheism and a judgment and heaven and hell, only to get for answer:

> *O my uncle, if they placed the sun on my right hand and the moon on my left, to force [another translator uses the word "induce" here] me to renounce my work, verily I would not desist therefrom until God made manifest His cause, or I perished in the attempt.*[1]

Mohammed was no charlatan. But beyond this, who or what he was, or what our opinion of him may be, is of little importance compared to what the present-day Moslem would like to think he was. Ameer Ali has written the following:

> *His singular elevation of mind, his extreme delicacy and refinement of feeling, his purity and truth, form the constant theme of the traditions. He was most indulgent to his inferiors, and would never allow his awkward little page to be scolded whatever he did. "Ten years," said Anas, his servant, "was I about the Prophet, and he never said as much as 'Uff' to me." He was very affectionate towards his family.... He was very fond of children. He would stop them in the streets, and pat their little cheeks. He never struck any one in his life. He never first withdrew his hand from another's palm, and turned not before the other had*

[1] Ameer Ali, *The Spirit of Islam* (London: The Christophers), p. 37.

*turned. His hand was the most generous, his breast the most
courageous, his tongue the most truthful; he was the most
faithful protector of those he protected; the sweetest and
most agreeable in conversation; those who saw him were
suddenly filled with reverence; those who came near him
loved him; they who described him would say, "I have
never seen his like, either before or after." He was of great
taciturnity; and when he spoke, he spoke with emphasis and
deliberation, and no one could ever forget what he said.
"Modesty and kindness, patience, self-denial, and generosity
pervaded his conduct, and riveted the affections of all
around him. With the bereaved and afflicted he sympathized
tenderly. . . . He shared his food even in times of scarcity
with others, and was sedulously solicitous for the personal
comfort of every one about him." His conduct towards the
bitterest of his enemies was marked by a noble clemency
and forbearance. Stern, almost to severity, to the enemies
of the State, mockings, affronts, outrages, and persecutions
towards himself were, in the hour of triumph . . . all buried
in oblivion, and forgiveness was extended to the worst
criminal. . . . He visited the sick . . . accepted the invitation
of a slave to dinner, mended his own clothes, milked his
goats, and waited upon himself. . . . The mind of this re-
markable Teacher was, in its intellectualism and progressive
ideals, essentially modern. Eternal "striving" was in his
teachings a necessity of human existence. . . . To him the
service of humanity was the highest act of devotion. His
call to the faithful was not to forsake those to whom they
owed a duty; but in the performance of that duty to earn
"merit" and reward.*[2]

Was Mohammed the paradigm of those statements? Was he an
ideal of warmth and tenderness and concern for friend and for slave,
generous and forgiving, tolerant of other faiths, an admirer of learning?
If such was the man Moslem leaders look up to as their model, then
from Islam, once its renaissance gets under way, should come many a
much-needed blessing and boon for mankind.

[2] *Ibid.*, pp. 118-120.

Critics of Islam have pointed with truth to the unenviable position of the Moslem woman; her status almost everywhere today, except in Java, Turkey, and lately in Egypt, is but little above that of the domestic animal. Among the Astrakans, for instance, a middle-aged man of wealth may have married and divorced as many as forty women; and a woman, through no choice of her own, since she does not have the right to initiate divorce proceedings, may have married and been divorced by as many as ten husbands during her years of greatest attractiveness. No Moslem woman, let it be said, can be forced into marriage against her will. Missionaries point with moral horror at the statement in the Koran permitting as many as four wives at a time. In respect to all this the educated Moslem will concede that the status of womankind in present day Islam leaves much to be desired. Her condition is not to be excused by the fact that Mohammed's teachings gave the woman of the Arab world of his day a vastly improved status. But think in larger terms, we are cautioned. Contrast the general attitude in Islam toward divorce and Islam's anything but monastic or Puritanical attitude toward the relations of man and wife, with those that are typical of the Christian. Consider the words of the church father, Tertullian, who saw in women "the devil's gateway, the unsealer of the forbidden tree, the deserter of the divine law, the destroyer of God's image — man." Or the great Chrysostom, for whom women were "a necessary evil, a natural temptation, a desirable calamity, a domestic peril, a deadly fascination, a painted ill." Consider the heights of esteem in which Christianity held asceticism, the thousands of monasteries and convents, the devastations of Puritanism, the sinfulness of sex, the difficulty and shame of divorce. Consider the situation in this larger perspective, we are told, and perhaps we will be somewhat more circumspect in condemning Moslem leniency and frank (and probably healthy) sensuousness. And while we are on the subject, don't overlook the further fact, the Moslem reminds us, that the source of the code of chivalry, medieval knight errantry, the chivalrous attitude toward womankind that raised Christian women above mere subservience, was none other than an aspect of Islamic culture — picked up in the East by the Crusaders, in the West from the Moors of Andalusia.

The emptiest and at the same time possibly one of the most telling accusations against Islam has been the popular one that Moslem women are supposed to have no souls. This calumny was answered by the

Prophet, who had been approached by an aged woman and asked how she could get to heaven. Mohammed is supposed to have replied brusquely that ugly old women never get to heaven. She burst out in tears and wailing. Then the Prophet continued, "Ugly old women never get to heaven, because at the gates of heaven God makes them all young and beautiful!"

The word "Islam" means submission — a fatalistic submission, in recent centuries at least, to sordid living conditions, sordid political conditions, sordid cultural conditions such as we of the West could never for one minute accept as the will of God. Our response to Moslem submission is that of Justice Douglas to children in the neighborhood of Damascus; children with "ringworms on their faces as big as saucers . . . little children whose faces were matted with flies feeding on open sores . . . no doctor, no first-aid station. . . ." No sanitation — "Village after village the same sight. . . ." How horrible! For us there is to be no submission to ringworm, to flies or sores or unsanitary conditions. In fact, it is difficult to conceive of anything an enterprising and humanitarian-minded American can think of submitting to any more: not poverty, not disease, not tyranny of man over man, not marriage wretchedness with the recourse now of divorce, not lower class obscurity, not occupational drudgery, not shortness of life, not ugly and colorless surroundings, not self-limitations as long as he can afford a psychoanalyst, not even worry or anxiety or unhappiness with the availability now of that miracle of all miracle drugs, the tranquilizing pill! Thanks to Western science and enterprise and humanitarian effort we are, to all intents and purposes, in actual possession of Aladdin's magic lamp. The good things that were only the dreams of the dreamers of the Arabian Nights are ours in reality. We sail through the air from continent to continent faster than the speed of wind and in objects that are of infinitely more traveling comfort than a seat on some flimsy old Oriental rug!

But with all our knowledge can we say that we have learned to live? With all our power have we found happiness? May it possibly be — and oh what heresy in the ears of a certain stripe of liberal are these words! — may it possibly be that there are still some immovable obstacles, some irresistible forces to which we must submit before we will learn how to live, before we will find happiness?

The typical Moslem submission to conditions that do not absolutely demand submission is one extreme. But equally in the extreme is the person who can't take anything uncomfortable or frustrating or intellectually disturbing or seemingly unfair as being somehow inevitable and in the nature of things, the will of God, as it were. We become ill or we suffer from fatigue or tension pains, and instead of accepting them and relaxing, we fight and tense ourselves against the unpleasant sensations. And in fighting them all we succeed in doing is to tense against tensions and multiply our miseries. We habitually allow ourselves to become irritated and angered about political events upon which our ill feeling cannot have the slightest effect. We elbow our frantic ways up the ladder of recognition and success, advertising ourselves in everything we do; laying waste our energies; alienating ourselves from our fellow men and losing the indispensable sustenance of their good will; forgetting the while that satisfaction in success can come only to the person whose success is achieved by virtue of that in him which floats him to his natural level in society, as the wood or the cork floats upward in the water. We struggle with the training and developing of our children until our very struggle produces mental malformations in them. We discipline ourselves, imagining that by discipline alone we can make anything we wish out of what we have, meanwhile becoming neurotics, failing to accept in ourselves that which we most uniquely and distinctively are. We fight advancing years; welcome every hour medical hygiene and vitamins can add to the prolongation of our youth; the while missing out on the major satisfactions of each of the several stages of life and of growing old artfully and gracefully. We shudder at the thought of anything to which we might have to surrender, as the Moslem surrenders to what he regards as the will of God.

Similar thoughts began to plague the mind of a young Englishman, the son of an Episcopalian clergyman, in the service of a raja in Malaya. He thought of his fellow Englishmen, and also of Americans — how they are driven mad at times by the pressures of all the things they feel they must do to keep from submitting to anything, "rushing about like madmen, up in the air one moment, down in the depths the next." And then he commented: "There were my Malays, calm and poised and dignified, accepting what came to them as the will of God."[3]

This Englishman, Chale, had occasion to spend a night with a

[3] Owen Ritter, *Triumphant Pilgrimage and English Muslim's Journey* (George G. Harrap, Ltd.).

young Moslem who was to die the next day for having killed a man for the sake of a girl with whom he had been passionately in love. From this Malay came never a word of complaint, no plea for mercy — only a quiet dignity. During the night Chale heard periodically: "Allah-u-Akbar" (God is the Greatest). Later, when being led before the firing squad, the name "Allah-u-Akbar," and the same quiet dignity. What this tortured young Moslem seemed to find in his faith was exactly what Chale knew he most needed: the peace of surrender to and the acceptance of that which is inevitable and in the nature of things.

It was a similar but somewhat nobler death that Justice Douglas described; that of a youth of Azerbaijan who had spoken up too frankly against the occupying Russian communists in the early 1940's. They forced him to dig his own grave and then proceeded, after they had tied him hand and foot, to bury him alive. But even in death he was not to be outdone. His shout and final words, muffled by the falling dirt, heard over and again, were to the effect that Allah is greater.

When tyranny and awful misfortune seem for the day and the week and the year to have taken over completely and absolutely, and the future holds no glimmer of tangible hope, and men go down in individual defeat, what strength and courage do they derive from the firm belief that this sort of thing is not grounded in the nature of things, and that it just can't go on forever?

Thoughts such as this led the young Englishman, Chale, to take the final step and become a Moslem. Also, paradoxically, these thoughts led him to the belief that in Islam and in Islam alone was the wherewithal for the removal of one of the most unendurable of all the evils with which mankind has been afflicted. This evil he saw eradicated as he sat on the deck of a Mecca-bound steamer. There were Turks in European suits, Syrians, wild-looking Afghanistan tribesmen with knives at their sides, cultivated Egyptians, Arabs, Moroccan Berbers, Chinese, Negroes from the hinterlands of Africa; each spreading his or her mat or mattress on the deck, making that spot his quarters. Next to him, black or yellow or gray or white — all of them, regardless of differences, were traveling in peace; all bound for the holy place of submission to the will of God who through their prophet commanded that all men should be brothers, not in word only, but in deed and in truth, and not only upon the crowded decks of the pilgrim steamer but also in everyday living in all their relations with one another.

From everywhere over the Moslem world come stirrings, as has been suggested, of a renaissance — a rebirth of science and learning, a keener aliveness than there has been in centuries to the words of the Prophet: "Seek knowledge, even if it is found in China." Everywhere, also — let us be realistic about it — is the resurgence of fanatical sects. But of vastly greater power and drive than the sects is the rise of that which is symbolized by the statue which stands in the station square in Cairo. It is a marble sphinx whose posture suggests to the beholder that it has been asleep but is now about to awaken. At the side of this sphinx stands that which would be most out of place in the Moslem world of the recent past — a woman. She is unveiled. She is beautiful. It is her outstretched hand (as it is now beginning to be outstretched in reality over the length and breadth of reawakening Islam) touching the sphinx that is bringing about at long last the opening of its eyes.

If there is one book in the whole of Oriental literature which one should read above all the others, it is, in my opinion, Laotse's Book of Tao. *If there is one book that can claim to interpret for us the spirit of the Orient, or that is necessary to the understanding of the characteristic Chinese behavior, including literally "the ways that are dark," it is the* Book of Tao. *For Laotse's book contains the first enunciated philosophy of camouflage in the world; it teaches the wisdom of appearing foolish, the success of appearing to fail, the strength of weakness and the advantage of lying low, the benefit of yielding to your adversary and the futility of contention for power. It accounts in fact for any mellowness that may be seen in Chinese social and individual behavior. If one reads enough of this book, one automatically acquires the habits and ways of the Chinese. I would go further and say that if I were asked what antidote could be found in Oriental literature and philosophy to cure this contentious modern world of its inveterate belief in force and struggle for power, I would name this book of "5,000 words" written some 2,400 years ago. For Laotse (born about B.C. 570) has the knack of making Hitler and other dreamers of world mastery appear foolish and ridiculous. The chaos of the modern world, I believe, is due to the total lack of a philosophy of the rhythm of life such as we find in Laotse and his brilliant disciple Chuangtse, or anything remotely resembling it. And furthermore, if there is one book advising against the multifarious activities and futile busy-ness of the modern man, I would again say it is Laotse's* Book of Tao. *It is one of the profoundest books in the world's philosophy.*

Lin Yutang, *The Wisdom of China and India*

Taoism: The Way of Wisdom and Peace

Who has not seen and admired those exquisite little Chinese landscape carvings that fit into a frame that can be hung from a wall: the gnarled, overhanging green trees; the moss-covered rocks; the waterfall; and in the midst of it all, the tiny pavilion or cave entrance in which sits the even more tiny contemplative communing with nature. This hermit, although he might be a Buddhist monk, is far more likely to be a Taoist recluse. And such, although he is not aware of it, has been the average person's introduction to Taoism.

It was to some such retreat of quiet majesty in the outdoors that old Laotze, the librarian and contemporary of Confucius and legendary founder of Taoism, was heading when he and the water buffalo on which he was riding were halted by the gatekeeper of the garrison at the pass that led from civilized China into the unknown country beyond the farthest border of the west. Behind him he was leaving his position as keeper of the royal library; behind him, the pomp and spendthrift luxury of the royal court; behind him, the greedy and lecherous local lords and those interminable intrigues and counter-intrigues, wars and assassinations, to which attention was called earlier in connection with the times of Confucius. The ancient Chow dynasty was in its last anarchical throes, decay and dissolution, and Laotze, which literally means "the old one," had had enough of it. To him the astonished gatekeeper, so goes the legend, put this request: "If you are going to disappear into retirement, Sir, will you not make a book for me?" In a few days, legend continues, the accommodating sage returned with the book, the Tao Te Ching, handed it to the officer, and then disappeared with his servant into the western mountain wilderness, never again to be heard from.

That he survived the rigors of primitive subsistence in a nature setting is more than likely. Taoist contemplatives are known even to this day for their expert knowledge of edible herbs and vegetables. But beyond survival, what did he find? What did he get from his com-

47

munions with nature? What was it that made others, by the thousands
and tens of thousands down through the centuries, follow his example;
establish themselves in wilderness hideaways; make themselves a favorite subject of Chinese folklore and art? Was all this mere sentimentality
and romanticizing? Was it escapism, the escapism everyone repeatedly
has to close his mind against when tempted with reveries of getting
away from the routine realities and enslaving responsibilities of civilized living; away to some Walden Pond, some gentleman farm, to an
early golf-and-fishing retirement? Or is there to be had from the Taoist
contemplative, as he insists, insights into that which is far more deeply
interfused in the world about us and in our own selves; a motion and a
spirit that can give us the strength to stand up to the responsibilities of
civilized life with some measure of pleasure in our hearts? These
insights *are* insights and not superficial truisms or preacherly moraliz-
ings. As insights they are not merely to be taken off the wall of the
antique shop of history and turned over and around and admired and
then put back with the comment, "How nice!" At this point one had
better add this further, parenthetical thought about Taoism: all Taoists
are not necessarily contemplatives and philosophers. There is much
about Taoism, as with every other religion, that is anything but admirable or full of insight. What is being presented in this book is simply
something of each religion at its most useful.

Man's relation to nature is as much of a problem and promise for
urban Americans today as it ever was for the ancient Chinese. Taoist
insights into both the problem and the promise of the nature relationship can best be introduced by a scene I caught out of the corner of my
eye, on a January trip, while speeding southward through Georgia. In
that scene I caught a vivid glimpse of the wrong kind of nature adjust-
ment, nature accommodation, nature communion. It is only in contrast
with this common and wrong kind of nature communion that the right
that is central in Taoism can be adequately appreciated.

It was a farm on a rise of ground of the southern edge of a
jungle-like tangle of bearded swampland. First in the order of appearance, the soil was more sand than soil; whitish, as if it were a field of
snow dirtied by weeks of settling dust and grime and wind-blown
debris. Then on a knoll, was the farmer's house. Its weather-beaten
appearance, the dark gray of its siding showing through paint that
once was white but now mostly peeled away, blended perfectly with its

dirtied wasteland surroundings. A story to the effect that the house had grown from some seed planted long seasons ago in that soil; that it had grown up along with the scrub oak and pine and old patches of dried weeds, would hardly have been beyond belief. Completing the picture of nature's taking over was the roof, with a patch or two of faded asphalt shingles blown into disarray by the wind; also, siding with its nails rusted away and hanging here and there from the walls in long, loose strips; porch and porch steps rotting and sagging toward the ground. This was the home, in all likelihood, of what has been called the Georgia "Cracker." In his accommodation to nature, his fitting into nature, the Cracker has let nature *take over*. He has let rain and wind and sun and rust and rot transform what was once a respectable house into a country slum hovel.

All this, of course, is only symbolic of a more subtle taking-over in the lives of these people. In that home the children, one would surmise, are trained to put up but little resistance to the pressures and wiles of nature as it whispers and pulls and prods from within. What they do with themselves in their little country schools and what comes of that schooling in a matter of months after graduation is only the psychological counterpart of the picture of the house they live in. Entirely foreign to their outlook is any such idea as going on to high school and then to training and professional school; on through years of disciplining and patient shaping of the stuff of nature into some kind of vocational competence and maturity. The urge is the very natural and powerful urge of the teen-age lad toward the teen-age girl, of the girl toward the lad; then, early marriage and a job — any kind of job. Next follows a baby and then more babies and the almost automatic stimulation of parental affection and devotion; then the greying of the hair and the slowing down; children in turn repeating the cycle, grandchildren. All in all, that lifetime, painted by a penetrating artist, could be typified by nothing quite so pictorially accurate as the weather-beaten house of the Georgia Cracker who has let nature take over. Giving in to nature as the Cracker gives in — failing to stand up to nature with paint and shingles and nails and schoolbooks and vocational training and marriage that is postponed until years of greater maturity — what is this but to invite degeneration and decay, or at best to make of the greatness of our endowments not persons of full manly or womanly stature, but instead mere dwarfs?

The lesson of the Georgia Cracker is clear: only to the extent that we stand up to nature with hammer and paint brush and textbook and schoolroom do we become fully human in body and heart and mind and spirit. Such was the teaching of Confucius and the Confucians. Out of the crude stuff that, left to itself, is the brawling teen-age gangster, the pinball machine and beer joint habitué, the howling male at the boxing match, the country bumpkin, the Confucian of today would make the respectable suburbanite with his garden and his do-it-yourself shop, the college graduate and hi-fi enthusiast — in a word, the Confucian gentleman. The good Confucian gentleman is very much concerned with public welfare. He stands up to nature in the raw in human affairs. And this very concern develops him, brings out his talents and whatever bigness or greatness he may have in him.

All this is well and good, all this standing up to nature. But keep on with this standing up to nature, says in effect the Taoist philosopher, and you'll get into trouble. Nature is not quite that simple and not that easily disposed of. Look farther into nature and there you will find something far more deeply interfused. You will find nature's way; what the Chinese call the Tao, the concept that is central in Taoism.

A case in point is described in a travel story written some 250 years ago by a Taoist philosopher. The traveler who is seeking Tao by way of wanderings in the out-of-doors describes an old man who has failed to look sufficiently deep into nature to find the Tao.

I sometimes see an old man with white hair on his head marching slowly with a stoop in an official procession, still clinging to these things and unwilling to let them go. If one day he quits office, he looks about with knitted eye-brows. Inquiring if the carirage is ready, he is still slow to depart, and passing out of the city gate of the capital, he still looks back. When back at his farm, he still disdains to occupy himself with planting rice and hemp and beans, and morning and night he will be asking for news from the capital. Or he will still be writing letters to his friends at the court, and such thoughts flit back and forth in his breast ceaselessly until he draws his last breath. Sometimes an Imperial order for his recall to office arrives at the moment when he is breathing his last, and sometimes the official messenger arrives with the news just a few hours after he closes his eyes. Isn't this ridiculous?[1]

How must one train himself, the question is asked, so that one can emancipate himself from such things in good time? All his life this official has stood up to nature. He has made nothing of the image of the contemplative sitting under green trees among huge rocks at the side of a waterfall. He knows nothing, consequently, of the sensuous satisfactions as well as of the peace of spirit that can come of going out into the field to plant rice or beans. And now, understandably, nature is kicking back and making him ridiculous.

The traveler, a Mingliaotse, is picked up by a young Confucian gentleman and invited to a picnic. It is the time of the year when the trees are arrayed in their new clothes of freshest green, when the air is fragrant with the perfume of blossoms and birds are outdoing themselves in song. They come to half a dozen Confucian scholars waiting for them under some cherry trees in full bloom on the bank of a river. With the passing of rice and wine the conversation becomes continuous and brilliant.

They pass witty remarks about the different people and the gentry. Some declaim poems celebrating the spring, some sing the song of gathering flowers, some discuss the policies of the court, and some tell of the secluded charm of hills and woods. There is then an exciting conversation going on, with each trying to outdo the others, while the Taoist merely occupies himself by his chewing rice.[2]

Finally they turn to Mingliaotse. How about something from the Taoist traveler? He doesn't tell them in so many words that they have carried their cultivation, their sophistication, their brilliance to the point where it has become artificial, an exhibition of rather petty egos, and where, because it is artificial, nature begins to kick back at them. He doesn't say to them directly that here in him is one who is more natural, more, as Mingliaotse put it elsewhere, in "harmony with" his "own original nature"; hence more profitable as a conversationalist and more

[1] Lin Yutang, *The Importance of Living* (The John Day Co.), pp. 355-356.
[2] *Ibid.*, p. 351.

desirable as a friend and a family man. But all this he conveys with the winning genuineness of the one who reflects the more profoundly natural. He says simply:

> *Why, I am just enjoying the many fine and wise things you gentlemen have been saying, and have not been able to understand them all. How can I contribute anything to your conversation?*[3]

Discipline, education and cultivation mean little or nothing unless with these desirable qualities or achievements is that certain indefinable naturalness that is suggested not only by Mingliaotse but also in the words of the Tao Te Ching:

> *On tiptoe your stance is unsteady;*
> *Long strides make your progress unsure;*
> *Show off and you get no attention;*
> *Your boasting will mean that you have failed;*
> *Asserting yourself brings no credit;*
> *Be proud and you will never lead.*[4]

> *To persons of the Way, these traits*
> *Are called "the dregs and tumors of Virtue,"*
> *Which are things of disgust.*
> *Therefore the man of Tao spurns them.*[5]

It is this indefinable but all-important naturalness, and with it the kind of communing with nature that saves the retired official from ridiculous anxiety, that the Taoist philosopher is forever trying to discover and make clear and real to himself.

One who has had this genuineness, this naturalness, seems to be able to get things done, the Taoists point out, with a certain effortlessness, as did the butcher who hadn't sharpened his knife for years. His blade was guided invariably to the soft spots, interstices in the knuckles and joints, never hacking and hewing with brute force, never hitting a bone. This same effortlessness one can see in nature, they insist, if one will

---

[3] *Ibid.*
[4] R. B. Blakney, *The Way of Life* (New American Library of World Literature, Inc.), p. 76.
[5] Lin Yutang, *The Wisdom of China and India* (Random House), p. 596.

look beyond the whirlwind or cloudburst, for instance, whose furies spend themselves in but a few riotous minutes or hours; look beyond to the smooth comings and goings of the sun and the eternal procession of the seasons, and, more especially, to the work of water, which supports the life of the fields and cuts valleys through the highest of mountains and hardest of ledges. Says the Tao Te Ching:

> Nothing is weaker than water,
> But water when it attacks something hard
> Or resistant, then nothing withstands it,
> And nothing will alter its way.[6]

Following the way of nature the wise man wins his battles without fighting, teaches without pounding anything into anyone's head, binds people to him in friendship without impressing them or pursuing them.

That the Taoist insights into the way of nature can incalculably enrich our daily living is borne out in the findings of present-day psychiatry. The person who stands in need of the psychiatrist is not one, ordinarily, who is lacking in discipline or education or cultivation. The chances are that he has had so much of working at shaping the stuff of heart and mind and muscle that he has become alienated from his true self. Alienated, he pushes himself or restrains himself or lays waste his energies in trying to keep the self he doesn't want to be in the background and the front-self he wants everybody to think he is in the foreground. He prods himself to concert pitch whenever he is with people. Then he suffers from the pains and aches of nervous tension, and then fights the pains and aches! Alienated from self he has no love for himself and, consequently, no real love for anyone else. Thus, this alienation inevitably brings alienation from friends, from wife or husband, from fellow men. He comes out lonely, erotically frustrated, alone against the world, uncertain, exhausted, sick. He is ripe for therapy. And what in essence is this therapy but an attempt to lead him back to an awareness and an appreciation of the ways of nature in himself? Back to the wild land of the id, to his own repressed appetites, erotic and murderous impulses; back to an awareness of all the sensations of life itself — conscious seeing, hearing, feeling and relaxing, as well as releasing restless energy. Therapy brings him back to

[6] R. B. Blakney, *op. cit.*, p. 131.

the natural; back to what the Taoist philosopher earlier quoted described as "harmony with" his own "original nature." With that
harmony re-established, he can go on to make the most of discipline
and education and cultivation. Established again in the Tao, as Taoist
philosophers would put it, one becomes a blessing not only to oneself
but also to others. Says the Tao Te Ching:

> *The highest goodness, water-like,*
> *Does good to everything and goes*
> *Unmurmuring to places men despise....*[7]

The Taoist philosopher would save us from no end of worries and
anxieties that take the joy out of living. Most persons, says the famous
Taoist Chuangtse, are like the huge bird that flew over his head as he
was hunting with a crossbow. It alighted in a nearby tree in the royal
park. There, unmindful of the approaching hunter and his arrows, it
moved its head slowly in the direction of a big mantis. The mantis, in
turn, was unaware of the bird. Its attention was on the cicada it had
caught and was about to devour. Then the royal gamekeeper came up
and all but accused the philosopher of being a poacher and a thief.
Chuangtse's comment was a question to the effect that, wasn't this what
we are all doing?

All of us are so intent on cicada or mantis or bird that we are
oblivious to the threats to our well-being and forget our real natures.
We fret about the latest in automobile design, in clothes styling, in
beautiful houses, in efficient kitchens and colorful bathrooms. It is
better, of course, that we do this — that we have a concern for order
and beauty and art — than that we should be like the Georgia Cracker
who has such little concern for the aesthetic. But in carrying these
interests to the wasteful extremes of today, are people not behaving like
the bird and the mantis? And like the monkeys that Chuangtse speaks
of? Their keeper, he wrote, gave each monkey three nuts in the morning and four at night. One among them raised a howl. Three in the
morning and four at night was not right! The keeper then proceeded
to give each four nuts in the morning and three at night. Then, although
the total number for each monkey remained the same, they were well
pleased. Three-in-the-morning last year's model clothes, three-in-the-

[7] R. B. Blakney, *op. cit.*, p. 60.

morning last year's model cars, three-in-the-morning houses. How un-
satisfactory! But let the monkey-keeper advertising men give the
hominoids the slightest change in styling — four nuts in the morning. . . ! What is this yearning for four nuts in the morning but a
neglect of our real natures? And even if all these newishly styled objects
are but symbols of status, as we may well be reminded, and even if
getting them assures status, what is this status? Isn't it like the entice-
ment that was held out to Chuangtse himself once when he was
fishing? To him came two messengers from the prince of Ch'u, with an
offer that would have delighted the heart of any Confucian gentleman.
The prince wanted him to take over the administration of his kingdom.
Chuangtse replied to the effect that he had heard that the prince owned
a sacred tortoise that had lived 3,000 years, and whose preserved remains
he kept carefully guarded in a chest in the ancestral temple.

"Would this tortoise," Chuangtse asked the messengers, "rather be
dead and have its remains venerated, or would it rather be alive and
wagging its tail in the mud?"

"Alive, of course," was the answer.

"Begone!" responded Chuangtse. "I too will wag my tail in the
mud."

One doubts if Chuangtse would have held that the administration
of the state is unimportant. He was merely dramatizing the fact that
there is in life something more important and more satisfying to acquire
and live for; something that would promote both peace and order in
the state — the finding and living of the Tao, living in the way of
naturalness.

No one can read in these philosophers, or read the paradoxes
and cryptic affirmations of the Tao Te Ching, without coming alive
to scores of insights and helpful everyday applications of the Taoist
philosophy. We shall concern ourselves with but an additional two
of the insights and applications, which should be of value for contemporary Americans.

The first of these is what the Taoist makes of death. This comes
out nicely in the story of the conduct of one of Laotze's followers at
his funeral. The account, of course, is pure fiction, but significant
nevertheless. This follower, Ch'in Yi, went to the rites, uttered three
yells, and departed. When asked about his conduct, so unbecoming to
a follower and friend of the great man, Ch'in answered:

When I went in to mourn, I found old persons weep-
ing as if for their children, young ones wailing as if for
their mothers. [Here were] words . . . and tears without
any intention. (To cry thus at one's death) is to evade the
natural principles (of life and death) and increase human
attachments, forgetting the source from which we receive
this life. . . . The Master came, because it was his time to be
born; he went, because it was his time to go away. Those
who accept the natural course and sequence of things and
live in obedience to it are beyond joy and sorrow. The
ancients spoke of this as the emancipation from bondage.[8]

The second of the helpful insights of Taoism has to do with such
things as the abortive revolution in Hungary or the disgraceful mis-
carriage of justice in Mississippi in connection with the murder of the
Negro lad, Emmett Till. Here are situations in which wrong seems
triumphant, and humanitarian-minded individuals can do nothing, or
next to nothing.

The revolution in Hungary reminded us that people by the hundreds of millions are still under a whiplash tyranny. That tyranny is
not new and it is not likely to collapse in the near future. To make
matters worse, we now have word — the word may be the usual propa-
ganda for further military appropriations, but it may also be true —
that this tyranny has become a technological giant armed with huge
fleets of submarines, jet bombers and intercontinental missiles, all
equipped with atomic explosives. Massing of brute might and demon-
strations of man's inhumanity to man were by no means unknown to
Taoists. They saw the Confucian scholars trying to grapple with these
ills and iron them out. But beyond the efforts of well-meaning scholars
and beyond the periodic resurgence of the ways of the jungle in human
affairs, the Taoist philosophers thought they saw the workings of a
higher order in the affairs of men. As a result of the workings of this
silent and invisible order, the rude and the untruthful and the brutal,
the philosophers pointed out, were brought to their ruin one by one.

A Stalin may rule by falsehood and terror for a few precarious
years, but his successors will necessarily find it difficult if not impossible
to follow in his steps. An Emmett Till may be murdered in Mississippi.

[8] Quoted in L. Yutang, *op. cit.,* pp. 644-645.

His self-confessed murderers may be brought into court. They may get the financial backing of neighbors and community, the defense of able lawyers. They may be acquitted and go free. One law for white and another for Negro — the grossest of discrimination. Atrocities and inequities like this were not unknown to the Taoist philosophers of antiquity. But here again they discerned the workings, behind the scenes of things, of a primordial and inexorable justice. This is what the *Look* magazine reporter, William Bradford Huie, uncovered one year after he had first interviewed the killers of Emmett Till, Roy Bryant and his half-brother, J. W. Milam.

Reporter Huie found, in talking with individuals in the community, "a strong sense of repugnance to the whole episode." What he got from the killers was word of "disillusionment, ingratitude, resentment, misfortune." During the course of the year the chain of stores owned and operated by the family was forced out of business. Negroes to whom they catered refused to buy from them. Bryant had to go to a veterans' school to rehabilitate himself vocationally by learning welding. Milam, who operates cotton-picking machines, had difficulty getting Negro help. White help, he found, is ruinously costly. Only with the utmost effort did he succeed in locating a piece of land he could rent for his cotton planting. Financial backing, his "furnish," had to come from outside the county. The county sheriff will no longer let Milam carry a pistol, which makes him all but an outcast. Milam, a desperately lonely and unhappy man, confessed to the reporter that he was "a man alone." "I don't know nobody and nobody knows me." He is an exile in his own home community. How many times in history have men chosen death in preference to this kind of ostracism! These two men, concluded the reporter, "will come to regard the dark morning of August 28, 1955, as the most unfortunate of their lives."

Operating in the nature of things, the Taoist philosopher assures us — sometimes hidden for years at a time, but there nevertheless — is some kind of great equilibrium that makes the victor never quite the victor and the defeated never wholly the defeated; the strong not as strong as he may think he is; the weak far from as weak as he may fear. For the wise and good man there is, therefore, the consolation and the assurance of that which is suggested in the story about an old man and his son and their horse, told by the Taoist philosopher Liehtse. One day the horse strayed away, apparently for good. When the neighbors came over to express their sympathy over this misfortune the old man replied, "How do you know this is bad fortune?" A few days later the horse returned, leading a number of wild horses. This time the neighbors came over with congratulations which the old man met with the protest: "How do you know this is good fortune?" Next one of the wild horses broke the son's leg as he tried to mount it. This called for further expressions of sympathy from the neighbors and the further response from the old man: "How do you know that this is bad fortune?" In a year war broke out and all the lads of the neighborhood, except the son with the crippled leg, were herded off to battle!

Far more effective than is commonly thought is a wondrous tendency toward equilibrium in the affairs of men and in nature; another aspect of what the Taoist calls the Tao, the way of nature. This way, if made the goal and rule of life, rewards one in a manner that recalls the words of Saint Paul: "To them that love God all things work together for good. . . ." Said Laotze:

> Once grasp the great Form without form,
> And you roam where you will
> With no evil to fear,
> Calm, peaceful, at ease.
>
> At music and viands
> The wayfarer stops.
> But the Way, when declared,
> Seems thin and so flavorless!
>
> It is nothing to look at
> And nothing to hear;
> But used, it will prove
> Inexhaustible.[9]

---

[9] R. B. Blakney, *op. cit.*, p. 88.

Zen seeks above all ... the concrete and the simple that lie beyond the snarled tangles of intellectualization. Zen is the concrete itself. Zen eschews abstractions, or uses them only to get beyond them. Even when Zen declares against abstractions, it has to put the matter concretely: thus when the great Master Tokusan has his enlightenment, he does not merely say in pallid fashion that concepts are not enough; no, he burns all his philosophic texts, declaring, "All our understanding of the abstractions of philosophy is like a single hair in the vastness of space." Let the Western reader fasten upon this image and he will find it harder to miss the point. Or when another Master remarks on the difficulty of solving one of the Zen questions — which is equivalent to answering the riddle of existence itself — he does not merely say it is difficult or so very, very difficult it is well-nigh impossible, but this: "It is like a mosquito trying to bite into an iron bull." The image lives because the image suggests the meaning beyond conceptualization.

This passion for the living fact accounts for that quality in the Zen masters which must seem most amazing to the Westerner: their supreme matter-of-factness. "What is the Tao (the way, the truth)?" asks the disciple. "Your everyday mind," replies the Master; and he goes on to amplify: "When I am hungry I eat; when tired, I sleep." The disciple is puzzled, and asks whether this is not what everybody else does too. No, the Master replies; most people are never wholly in what they are doing; when eating, they may be absent-mindedly preoccupied with a thousand different fantasies; when sleeping, they are not sleeping.

William Barrett, *Zen Buddhism: Selected Writings of Suzuki*

The Humanistic Mysticism of Zen Buddhism

Among all the world's great religions there is none whose proponents are more confident that they have something of inestimable help for modern man than are the devotees of Zen Buddhism. Their confidence is strongly bolstered by the widespread quickening of interest in this faith. Its most prominent representative in this country, the distinguished Diasetz Suzuki (born in 1869), is winning an ever-increasing audience both for his lectures in Columbia University and for the many writings in which he advocates the principles of Zen with the enthusiasm and assurance of a missionary. Get the Zen vision, he promises, and "All your mental activities will now be working to a different key, which will be more satisfying, more peaceful, and fuller of joy than anything you ever experienced before. The tone of life will be altered. There is something rejuvenating in the possession of Zen. The spring flowers look prettier, and the mountain stream runs cooler and more transparent."[1]

As the news magazine *Time* brought out in a two-column article on Zen (in the February 4, 1957 issue), the First Zen Institute of America is holding three well-attended meetings a week in Manhattan. In Kyoto, an old center of Zen in Japan, an institute was opened early in 1957 for Westerners who wish to partake of the benefits of this faith. The latest report is that a new meditation hall is being built to accommodate the influx of students from the United States. These aren't the first Americans who have recognized the value of Zen. Among others is Northwestern University's William Montgomery McGovern, who several years ago was listed by *Life* magazine as one of the ten most successful university professors in America. McGovern at one time became a Buddhist monk and was admitted to the priesthood. It was he who first interested me in the possibilities of Zen; and it was in his

[1] Diasetz Suzuki, *An Introduction to Zen Buddhism* (Doubleday & Co.), p. 97.

60

home, some twenty years ago, that I met Suzuki. In more recent years the late Karen Horney, world famous psychiatrist, became passionately interested in Zen, even to the point of going to Japan to learn about it firsthand in the monasteries. In the religion she found a marked possibility for "self-realization without either the false image of an idealized self, or without the resigned and dependent clinging to external props like family, social group, or church." The psychiatrist C. G. Jung suggests in the chapter he wrote as preface to Suzuki's book, *An Introduction to Zen Buddhism,* that in this religion's pursuit of psychological wholeness are great therapeutic possibilities.

One can measure the possible impact of Zen on the Western world only when he has some idea of its multiple effects on Japan and the Japanese. To bring out that in Japan the three sects of Zen — Rinzai, Soto, and Obaku — have more than twenty thousand temples; that the temple compounds are spots of appealing beauty where there are likely to be swings and games for children who flock there to play; that the Zen monastery is likely to be equipped with telephone and, in its kitchen, electric ranges; and that monks are free to marry and have families if they so choose, would give but little idea of the place this religion occupies in the total life of the Japanese. Introduced to Japan from China roughly about 1200 A.D., it enjoyed an almost immediate popularity among the aristocratic and military classes. And it seems to have enjoyed this popularity without becoming worldly and avaricious, as did Christian monasticism in Europe, and without in itself becoming militaristic, as did European Christianity. It was to the Zen monk and priest that the soldier came to learn how to meet danger as had the Zen monks who met death in the flames of a monastery, which in the course of a civil war had been surrounded by soldiers and set on fire. As the abbot was about to die in the flames he was heard calmly composing a poem to the effect that even fire is cold to the mind that thinks it is. A soldier coming to a Zen master with the word that he is about to go through a most critical period and asking what he should do, would be answered: "Go straight ahead, and no looking backward!" Zen, moreover, provided the frame of mind that those who followed the art of fencing found not only helpful but indispensable.

This frame of mind or attitude, so helpful in facing up to the perils both of war and of fencing, was not mere reckless abandon but

was an outcome of a new insight into the nature of self. It came also
of a new insight into the nature of the world of nature. This is implied
in the answer made by a Zen master to a Confucian friend who had
asked to be shown the way to Zen enlightenment: "Do you hear the
murmuring sound of the mountain stream?" The Confucian answered
that he did. "There," said the Master, "is the entrance."

Out of Zen's new kinship with and appreciation of nature came
the sensitive new painting known as the Sumiye sketch, and also the
new poetry of the Haiku. The idea was to catch the aesthetic impression
with the fewest possible strokes of a brush, the fewest words. Zen
became the fountainhead of higher and lower education in Japan. A
Japanese professor wrote:

> *The influence of Zen pervaded the lives of the people
> and moulded their perceptions in every branch of art — in
> the composition of poems, the building of houses and fur-
> nishing of rooms; in methods of flower arrangement, of
> gardening, and even of preparing and drinking tea. Indeed,
> there is in Japan hardly a form of thought or activity that
> Zen has not touched and inspired with its ideal of simple
> beauty. Fans . . . calligraphy, the Japanese smile, the stern-
> ness of expression, everything now known as peculiarly
> Japanese was the product of Zen, directly or indirectly.*[2]

We come now to the question that will put up with postpone-
ment no longer: "What, pray tell, is Zen Buddhism?"

The question, put to a Zen abbot, would probably get in answer
something like this: "Zen is really quite simple — once you get the
idea. It is the discovery of the Buddha nature in your own self and
in the world about you. That is all."

Those who were raised on the Christian New Testament would
probably go on to say to our Zen abbot: "Oh, I think I get it. What
you say about finding the Buddha nature in one's self reminds me of the
words of Saint Paul after his conversion. He wrote that he had become
a new man in Christ; that it was no longer Paul that lived, but Christ
who lived in him. To such a degree was he possessed by the spirit of
Christ — a spirit that was supposed to be very much alive and a real

[2] Quoted in J. B. Pratt, *Pilgrimage of Buddhism* (Macmillan Co.), p. 491.

presence in religious meetings — that Christ had taken over and literally had become his new self. If Paul had been converted to Buddhism would he not have written that he had become a new man in the Buddha and that it was no longer he that lived but the Buddha who lived in him?"

Before we had finished the abbot would be shaking his head. Finally he would burst in with a "No! No! No! You're decidedly on the wrong track. You are thinking of the *man* Buddha — Siddhartha — as if he were a Christ. Siddhartha is dead. His spirit is also dead. Dead, I tell you! There is no resurrected spirit of the Buddha to possess you and to take the place of your old self. When we talk about the Buddha nature," the abbot continues, "what we mean is not the spirit of the man Siddhartha, but exactly what the word 'Buddha' connotes: Enlightened One, which is to say, *Enlightenment.* You will find the Buddha or enlightened nature in yourself only when you have this enlightenment, when you have experienced Satori, as we Zens express it. When enlightenment has come to you then the world about you will seem different and *it also will be part of and share in this enlightenment."*

"Very well," we protest, "let's face it, we got off to a wrong start. Suppose we begin again, this time with the question: 'What is this enlightenment, this Satori? How do you go about getting it?' "

The abbot smiles reassuringly: "You didn't get off to a totally wrong start, really. Your bringing the ideas of Saint Paul into the picture has not been amiss. It has helped to bring out how utterly different is Zen from anything you have ever thought of in connection with religion. The next step toward Satori is to go beyond any ideas of God that may stand between you and your perception of the universe as it is: beyond God as a loving father looking after you, God as the source of ethics and conscience, and, most of all, beyond God as the Creator. See yourself the complete skeptic, looking up into the astronomical spaces of the skies and down into the cloud-chamber recesses of the incredibly small in the atom; see yourself beholding realities that are beyond explanation by any concept of a creator God, by any system of metaphysics, or even by the latest theories and concepts of the sciences."

It is at this point where Zen takes off; where one finds the humanistic doubter, the thoroughgoing skeptic and agnostic, face to face with a universe for which there is no adequate accounting, face to face with life and mind and consciousness for which there are also no final explanations, staring speechless into fog banks of unutterable and eternal mystery. The mood is the questing loneliness, the "Sabi" mood of the Japanese poem inspired by the familiar pictures of the monk who stands gazing at the Olympian summit of Fujiyama in the distance:

> *The wind-blown*
> *Smoke of Mt. Fuji*
> *Disappearing far beyond!*
> *Who knows the destiny*
> *Of my thought wandering away with it?*[3]

Knowing enough to know, at least abstractly, that things are not as they seem, we are perhaps somewhat better prepared for Zen than was the ordinary Japanese citizen of 1200 A.D., or the Chinese of around 600 A.D., when these ideas first appeared in China. To them water was water and not what it is to us: a combination of two gases, hydrogen and oxygen; the hydrogen and oxygen, in turn, combinations of electrons and protons; these, in turn, combinations of something even more elemental whose mystery we gloss over by giving it the commonplace label, "energy." To the medieval Chinese or Japanese a rock was no more than a rock and the sky was little more than an inverted blue bowl of sky. Self, similarly, was only self, a temporarily embodied spirit, and not what it is to us: the unaccountably complex and malleable form of an unaccountably mysterious something labeled "consciousness."

Those for whom water is merely water, rock merely rock, sky merely sky, and self merely self inevitably find themselves in the state of mind that is nowhere better expressed than in the first chapter of Ecclesiastes:

> *What profit hath man of all his labor wherein he laboreth under the sun? One generation goeth, and another generation cometh; but the earth abideth for ever. The sun also ariseth, and the sun goeth down, and hasteneth to its place where it ariseth. The wind goeth toward the south, and turneth about unto the north; it turneth about continu-*

---

[3] William Barrett, ed., *Zen Buddhism: Selected Writings of Suzuki* (Doubleday & Co.), p. 285.

ally in its course, and the wind returneth again to its circuits. All the rivers run into the sea, yet the sea is not full; unto the place whither the rivers go, thither they go again. All things are full of weariness; man cannot utter it: the eye is not satisfied with seeing, nor the ear filled with hearing. That which hath been is that which shall be; and that which hath been done is that which shall be done: and there is no new thing under the sun.

In medieval times there were thinking Chinese and thinking Japanese who were very much aware of the fact that things are not as they seem; that for those who can think beyond surface appearances, and in the mind's eye see everything under the aspect of infinitude, there is no boredom and no weariness, and all things under the sun are new and fresh. This, as has been suggested, we today know abstractly, intellectually. But it is one thing to know abstractly and intellectually and it is quite another to have a vivid firsthand experience of water or mountain or sky or self in its plenitude of mystery. The scientific facts we pile up, the logical theories and hypotheses we concoct never add up to the real thing; to the water we drink or swim in, to the night skies and the galaxies at which we gaze, to the self that loves and craves above all else to be loved. And who has not observed, about the abstract thinker — the man with all the facts, that the more he immerses himself in fact and theory and the more precisely he thinks and talks in terms of logic and mathematics, the more likely is he to remove himself from the real and from life itself, the more naive he becomes?

It is here that Zen invites us to go on to experience at first-hand, the supreme truth that all things are not as they seem. The abbot points out that looming up between us and the experience of things and of self in their infinitude are our superficial habits of thought, our conventional notions of things. These habits and these notions must be jarred, shocked, or blasted away if we are to achieve enlightenment.

"Very well," we say to our abbot friend, "blast away. What next?"

He responds with the suggestion that we try a "Koan" — which is to say, try one of the 1700 Zen thought-problems that are supposed to help the thinker get beyond his superficial habits of thought and his conventional notions of things, to the frame of mind which is receptive to the absolute mystery of all existence.

We get our Koan, our thought-problem thus: the abbot claps his hands together and asks if we hear it. The answer is, of course, a "Yes." Then he makes the same motion as before, but with the left hand only. His left hand beats the air soundlessly. Again he asks, "Did you hear that?" The answer this time is a "No." "Well," says our instructor, "listen until you do."

Meditate on this logically impossible problem long enough, days, months, even years, and the time will come when suddenly the limitations of logic and conventional notions drop away and the meditator finds himself open to the inexplicable wonder and majesty of the real that is flooding in upon him. If the illumination is too slow in coming the abbot might help him along some day by turning on him in the course of a quiet conversation and screaming in his ear, with all possible lung power, the meaningless word, "Kwats!" Or, again, he might suddenly, and on no provocation whatsoever, do the thing that is the absolute contradiction of the Buddhist code — quickly give the disciple a couple of resounding slaps in his face. Thus, by way of totally illogical and uncalled-for behavior, his mind is jarred for the moment. It is only in this moment — a fearsome moment that calls for the utmost of courage, Zens admit — when what makes for sanity in our grasp of the everyday and commonplace world of appearances seems about to take leave of us, when the head swims and we hardly know real from unreal, good from bad, self from not-self, that we are opened to the vision of a beyond that is the beyond near at hand and makes all things new.

The impression one gets from writers about Zen, and from Zen writers themselves, is that its central idea is all but impossible for the Western mind to grasp, that it is foreign to anything in our everyday experience. About the difficulties of Zen the learned J. B. Pratt wrote:

> It is with much hesitancy that I deal with the mysticism and the philosophy of Zen. There is no other subject connected with Buddhism so difficult for a Westerner to handle intelligently, no other so intangible, so different from everything with which we are acquainted, so hard to make plausible, so unspeakably queer.[4]

This point of view I can accept only in part. True, I have not

4 J. B. Pratt, op. cit., p. 623.

experienced Satori; I have not heard the clap of one hand batting the air. But is there anyone who has lived through a profound emotional crisis who has not experienced enough psychic unsettlement and disruption of our neat little world of the habitual and the abstract and the logical to have had some idea of the sense of the illimitable and the indescribable that can come to one at such times? How strange our own neighborhoods can suddenly appear to us! What an eerie world is revealed of a sudden when someone who has been with us and who has loved us and been loved by us is taken by death! And this same strange universe we have looked into when love has gone on the rocks, or when we have found ourselves alone like a child lost in the woods at night, or come to that place in life where Destiny says icily to our most cherished ambitions or hopes, "Thus far and no farther are *you* to go." Such occasions, and the anticipation of such occasions, frighten us. What we most fear about them is the psychic unsettlement that makes one into somebody not himself; the feeling that one's sanity is all but reeling and floored to the count of ten. But from the Zen Buddhist comes the word of consolation and assurance, that these experiences, however rough they may be at the time, are not to be dreaded. They are to be looked forward to and cherished as steps toward a fuller appreciation of that magnificence which is so profoundly a part of the world about us and of our own selves. They are but the preface to a greater illumination that fills one with the exultation one finds in that poet who is so much the kindred spirit of Zen in America, Walt Whitman (in his "Song of Myself"):

> *Stop this day and night with me and you shall possess the*
> *origin of all poems,*
> *You shall possess the good of the earth and sun (there are*
> *millions of suns left),*
> *You shall no longer take things at second or third hand, nor*
> *look through the eyes of the dead, nor feed on the*
> *spectres in books,*
> *You shall not look through my eyes either, nor take things*
> *from me,*
> *You shall listen to all sides and filter them from yourself.*

In the act of snapping out of the old habit of seeing and feeling everything through the observations of others and living only on the surface of things, one also snaps out of the old self that up to this moment has been the self of the conventional notion of self. Up to this moment one's major interest may have been working at the building, the integrating, the defending of that self. This ego-image he has made by piecing together secondhand what has appealed to him in the egos of others, as well as what he may have felt was useful or irrepressible among the psychological odds and ends of his own happenstance thoughts, feelings and adolescent ambitions. In this process of ego-construction he has also shouted down and repressed a multitude of impulses and yearnings and proddings that would make themselves features of his ego-face. He has struggled manfully with the mind, to keep it from wandering, always at a focus; closing eyes and ears and all sense organs to the throng of interests within and without clamoring for a voice in the deliberations of self. What a weird combination of models and rejected materials of psyche is the usual run of ego-image!

It is into this workshop of self-making that the Zens and Carl Jung enter with the well-taken protest that our ego-constructions, however attractive and impressive they may be to some, are utterly inadequate representations or expressions of the awesome totality that anyone actually is in his psycho-physical, conscious and unconscious wholeness. C. G. Jung, in the preface to Suzuki's *An Introduction to Zen Buddhism*, wrote:

> *This world of consciousness is inevitably full of restrictions, of walls blocking the way. . . . If the fragments offered by, or forced up from, the unconscious are successfully built into the life of the conscious, a psychic existence form results, which corresponds better to the whole of the individual personality, and therefore abolishes fruitless conflict between the conscious and the unconscious personality. Modern psychotherapy rests upon this principle, inasmuch as it was able to break away from the historic prejudice that the unconscious harbours only infantile and morally inferior contents. . . . The unconscious is the matrix of all metaphysical assertions, of all mythology, all philosophy (insofar as it is not merely critical) and all forms of life which are based upon psychological suppositions.*

To realize this more inclusive unity of conscious and unconscious, to be more the whole person, we need, says Suzuki, the Zen illumination which "breaks the ego-shell." We see this breaking of the ego-shell in part, at least, in Socrates' being ridiculed before a huge gathering in a play by Aristophanes. The famous dramatist had not overlooked Socrates' grotesque face, his pelican-like grace. The philosopher could have responded by becoming more intensely the little ego of one who is hurt — defiant, swearing eternal vengeance or running away. But not so with this man. The ego of everyday and commonplace identification didn't mean that much to him. To break out of his ego-shell was not too shattering. He did so, answering the ridicule and the howls by standing up to give everybody a good look at the one Aristophanes had set out to portray as a fool, thereby becoming, through that act, a bigger person than his antagonist.

It is in the more profound and cataclysmic breaking of the ego-shell, by way of a Zen-like illumination, that Carl Jung sees the possibility of a coming together of the unconscious and the conscious into a vastly richer and more healthy selfhood — a selfhood that is aware that the infinitude within is a product of and one with the infinitude of all that splendor of mystery and wonder we sense with the poet Blake, who saw a world in a grain of sand, a heaven in a wild flower and who held infinity in the palm of his hand.

This business of breaking the ego-shell, far from being farfetched and merely mystical, is as practical, as the ably written article in *Time* magazine observed, as a Mack truck. It makes, among other things, for the ego-lessness of the swordsman who is lost if at any split second his thought becomes centered on himself or on the impression he may be making. The attention must be selflessly fixed on the motions of the opponent. "You must follow the movement of the sword in the hands of the enemy," writes the Zen instructor,[5] "leaving your mind free to make its own counter-movement without your interfering deliberation. You move as the opponent moves, and it will result in his own defeat."

The several foregoing ideas are summarized, in a manner, in a Zen Buddhist writing of Chinese origin that reminds one of Christian in Bunyan's *Pilgrim's Progress*. The Zen pilgrim has been told that he will never find the satisfying life until he discovers the true nature of his self; until he has the illumination that shows him that the self, the eating, planting, counting self he has always thought of as self, is not his true being. In the story are ten pictures. Various scenes show the

[5] William Barrett, *op. cit.*, p. 291.

pilgrim engrossed in problems of this world, then his questing, and then his throwing aside all cares and meditating on ultimate questions. Finally comes the illumination. For a brief hour the logical and habitual world of space and time is destroyed, and his mind is opened to the infinitude beyond the seeming. He then comes back to familiar scenes and familiar people. This picture, the tenth, is entitled "Entering the city with bliss-bestowing hands. Below the drawing of the happy pilgrim are these lines:

> *Bare of foot and of chest, he*
> *mingles with the people of the*
> *market place;*
> *For aught of the grime and tatter of*
> *his garments,*
> *how blissful is his smile!*
> *He needs not the miracle-working*
> *magic of the divine ones;*
> *He has but to touch, and the barren*
> *trees are again in blossom.*[6]

There is no actual blooming of barren trees, of course; but seeing, as he does in effect, beyond the mere seeming, what he sees is as if the trees were truly in full bloom.

"Before a man studies Zen," goes a quotation from one of their writings, "mountains are mountains to him, waters are waters. But when he obtains a glimpse into the truth . . . through the instruction of a good Master, mountains are no longer mountains, nor waters waters." Later, after he has returned to his everyday chores and minglings with people, "mountains," continues the Zen quotation, "are again mountains and waters waters."[7]

When mountains become mountains again and waters waters one is left singing with the Zen poet:

> *How wondrously strange, how miraculous this!*
> *I draw water, I carry fuel.*[8]

Yes, the simplest and most commonplace of activities, even the lifting of a finger, as the Zens say, echoing Walt Whitman, how wondrously strange, how miraculous this!

[6] "The Ten Ox-Herding Pictures," a Zen poem.
[7] William Barrett, *op. cit.,* p. 14.
[8] Diasetz Suzuki, *op. cit.,* p. 83.

Throughout all of the history of our faith there has been an evolutionary development, on the one hand, providing a steady sophistication of ideas about man, God and religion (starting with sacrificial slaying and coming up to modern universal Judaism); on the other hand, there has been the continuing conflict which can be simplified for the moment as the struggle between the priest and the prophet. In every age, from the Biblical to the present, there have been counterparts of the priests and the prophets; there have been those who wanted a nationalistic, segregationalist and folkist type of religion which involved much of one's secular life as well as one's spiritual aspirations; but there have also been others who sought to distill the essence of Judaism and produce a religion linked to man and God rather than to land and blood.

Leonard R. Sussman,
Executive Director of the American Council for Judaism

Judaism at Its Best

In an article in *The Humanist* (No. 2, 1957) our era was called "The Century of the Homeless Man." The author, who dealt ably with the plight of the world's 17,000,000 homeless Germans, Jews, Arabs, Hindus, and Pakistanis, might well have proceeded to a companion article on the essential homelessness of a billion or more of the rest of us in this century. Most Americans are refugees, now in the second and third generation, from the old-style, nearly self-sufficient farm and its rootage of security in the good earth. One can return to the farm only if he has the means for a considerable investment in a tractor and numerous other costly pieces of farm machinery, as well as the agricultural know-how and a market sense and the venturesomeness to take a flier in some kind of farm specialization; which is to take a flier in more of the same bustle of business competition we know from day to day in the city. We who are in the suburbs are refugees from the city, and refugees to an extent that no trees or gardens or village atmosphere can make up for. The flight of communal leadership to the suburbs in turn makes the existence of those who live within the borders of our sprawling and slummy cities artificial to the point that they, too, are refugees. We are refugees in our own homes, refugees from the hominess of everything with the patina of the oldish and worn and lived-in, camped down in department-store-window surroundings amid the latest in interior swank, invention in furniture design, surrealistic painting and kitchen gadgetry — all of which is outdated in a decade. In our home communities, wherever we might be, we are refugees. Our homes, our cities and our suburbs are nothing but the flimsiest of camps. There we await our cells in the underground burrows which will be prepared for the onset of atomic warheads that will proceed to disintegrate and obliterate with soundless speed. We are refugees in the new universe that daily becomes larger by millions of light years; its atoms every day more complex and more promising and more terrifying. And man himself? What is he with the props of character pulled out from under him by the sudden obsolescence of so many virtues that once were one with the age-old age-of-scarcity? And now, the onset of the plenty that in the past has so regularly spelled flabbiness, gluttony, sensuality and disintegration for the privileged few. What is man? Put together the recent answers of Freud, Jung, Adler, Horney, Fromm, Tillich, Buber, and as many other thinkers, and what have we?

> *For men are homesick in their homes,*
> *And strangers under the sun,*
> *And they lay their heads in a foreign land*
> *Whenever the day is done.*[1]

We are truly a generation of homeless men and women. To this plaint I can picture many a Jew smiling knowingly and nodding his head and commenting: "Century of the Homeless Man! Suppose you had been homeless for twenty centuries! How would you like that?"

That there must be something of value in a religion that has carried its devotees through more than 2,000 years of homelessness is all but self-evident. That it had insights of incalculable value for the Western and Gentile world was the clear verdict of the Greco-Roman civilization of the time of Christ. That Judaism in its later rabbinical and talmudic developments has much of value for us is also the case, although not so commonly appreciated. To all this we shall return in but a few paragraphs. First, by way of introducing what Judaism has for us, we would do well to give consideration to a few indications of the more ancient and at the same time little-appreciated background of our Judaic heritage. In this perspective Judaism is seen as a sieve and funnel, as it were, through which the Western world has received much of the best of the ancient Egyptian and Semitic civilizations.

The modern reader need hardly be reminded that no small part of the Mosaic code goes back to the Babylonians and to the code King Hammurabi is supposed to have received from the Sun God, some 1800 years before Christ. It did not come, as Cecil B. deMille and the Book of Exodus so melodramatically put it, out of lightnings and thunderings and quakings of the earth, midst of which the voice of the God of the universe gave the law to Moses for all time to come. Much of what is good and wise in the Bible comes of the culture which

---

[1] Willard L. Sperry, *Reality in Worship* (Macmillan Co.), p. 61.

the barbarian Jews, then known as the Habiru, took over in about 1350 B.C. from the Canaanites, who in turn had been the recipients of the rich cultures of the Hittites, Amorites, Assyrians, Phoenicians, Babylonians and Egyptians. The Bible stories of Creation and the Flood are of Canaanitic or Babylonian origin. Psalm twenty-nine is based upon a Phoenician hymn. Passages in the Prophets themselves can be traced to these earlier sources. The hundred and fourth Psalm is in all likelihood derived from Pharaoh Ikhnaton's "Hymn to the Sun." The Jewish festivals are almost all of Canaanitic and seasonal origin; nature festivals. Even the Sabbath is Babylonian in word and rootage.

The worship of the golden calf — to which the people turned when Moses appeared to be lost among the clouds of Mt. Sinai, and which, according to legend, aroused Moses to punish 3,000 of his apostatizing fellow-Israelites by putting them to death by the sword — came of ancient Canaanitic fertility cults. And the worship of the calf, more specifically the bull, was later associated in northern Israel with the idea of Yahweh, Moses notwithstanding. This continued through the reigns of David and Solomon, even until Israel's fall to the Assyrians in 722 B.C., some 500 years after the death of Moses. The serpent of Moses was also a fertility cult symbol and was associated with the worship of Yahweh. It is quite possible that originally it was the bronze serpent, rather than any sacred tablets of the law, that was housed so reverently in the Ark. It is known that incense was offered to this serpent in the Temple at Jerusalem down to the time of King Hezekiah, contemporary of the prophets Micah and Isaiah, who, shortly before 700 B.C., ordered its destruction.

The very name Moses is not Hebrew but Egyptian. Similarly with the names of the Levites who were Moses' right-hand men when it came to punishing the 3,000 Israelites with death at Sinai. Names prominent among the Levites are Egyptian. Among other tribes there are no Egyptian names. All of which ties in with the further fact that at least 100 years before Moses led his fellow tribesmen, probably only the Levites, out of Egypt, other fellow-tribesmen of the Habiru had not only invaded Palestine but were intrenched and settled down in the north. There they were nicely on the way to adopting the Canaanite mores as well as writing which is the Hebrew script of today.

The land which the Habiru occupied was ideally suited to the creation of a people that was destined to be homeless for ages to come.

Theirs was to be the lot of the Canaanites they themselves had conquered and absorbed: always someone pressing in on that so-called
Promised Land, forming as it does a highroad between outreaching
empires to the north and to the south and the east: Assyria, Egypt,
Babylon, Persia, Greece, Rome, Islam — even to this very hour, with
Russia and Syria pressing down from the north, Jordan from the East,
and Egypt again from the south. Never, except for a few brief and
chaotic and widely separated centuries, was there a chance for any people
occupying that hapless country to get comfortably settled down in a
home land they could call their very own.

To the Jew being ground (as it was inevitable in Palestine that
he would be ground) between the upper and lower millstones of world
events everything was dark. He remembered the words of Amos, the
herdsman and prophet of Tekoa: "Woe unto you who are at ease, in
Zion," he had said to the rich of the northern kingdom. Woe to you
who "lie upon beds of ivory" and "stretch yourselves on couches, and
eat the lambs out of the flock . . . who tread upon the poor . . . sell
the poor for silver and the needy for a pair of shoes." Amos foretold
captivity and a day of darkness, "even very dark and no brightness in
it." The Jew remembered similar warnings from Isaiah, some years
later, to the people of the south in Judea; his insisting in no uncertain
terms that the day was at hand when they would lose the

> *tinkling adornments about their feet, and their cauls, the*
> *chains, and the bracelets, and the mufflers, the bonnets, and*
> *the ornaments of the legs and the headbands, and the tab-*
> *lets, and the earrings, the rings, and nose jewels, the*
> *changeable suits of apparel, and the mantles, and the*
> *wimples, and the crisping pins, the glasses, and the fine*
> *linen, and the hoods, and the veils. And it shall come*
> *to pass, that instead of sweet smell there shall be stink;*
> *and instead of a girdle a rent; and instead of a stomacher*
> *a girdling of sackcloth; and burning instead of beauty.*
> *Thy men shall fall by the sword . . . and in that day seven*
> *women shall take hold of one man. . . .*[2]

The Jew remembered how Assyria had pounced upon the northern

[2] Isaiah 3.

kingdom of Israel in 722 B.C., and how in but little more than a century, in 586, Babylon overran Judea and Jerusalem. The judgment of the prophets had come. The wicked had been brought low. Their homes had been burned, their babes dashed against stones, their wives taken for concubines, their men literally skinned alive. Their dismembered limbs make the gory heaps that are to be seen today carved in relief on the thrones of the Assyrian kings. But this judgment had been visited not merely upon those who sold the needy for a pair of shoes, whose wives fattened in idle luxury while others starved. It had come alike to all, to poor and righteous as well as to rich and callous. How could this be justice? Righteous judgment? Little wonder they wrote:

> By the rivers of Babylon, there we sat down, yea, we wept,
>   when we remembered Zion.
> We hanged our harps upon the willows in the midst thereof.
> For they that carried us away captive required of us a song;
>   and they that wasted us required of us mirth, saying,
>   Sing us one of the songs of Zion.
> How shall we sing the Lord's song in a strange land?[3]

When the land is strange, and every person and every object in one's surroundings wears also that gray and cowled cloak of strangeness, how can one sing? The world in this guise and the effects of such an appearance upon one were described by another Judean:

> We look for light, but behold darkness.
> For brightness, but we walk in gloom.
> We grope for the wall like the blind;
> Yea, as they who have no eyes, do we grope;
> We stumble at noonday as in the twilight;
> We are in dark places like the dead.
> We all growl like bears,
> And mourn sore like doves;
> We look for right, but there is none;
> For deliverance, but it is far from us.[4]

Then from yet another of the prophets of Judaism there came to

[3] Psalm 137.
[4] Isaiah 59.

the despairing Jew word to this effect: To all appearances everything is dark and there is no brightness to be seen on any horizon. But all this is only appearance, for behind the scenes, deeper in nature than you can know, is more than you think; some kind of order, some kind of power, a creative destiny that cannot get anywhere without human help, without the cooperation of persons who are willing to suffer persecution and indignities and homelessness and loneliness. And all this will be to the end of making it

> come to pass in the latter days, that the mountain of
> Jehovah's house shall be established on the top of the moun-
> tains, and shall be exalted above the hills; and all nations
> shall flow unto it. And many peoples shall go and say,
> Come ye, and let us go up to the mountain of Jehovah, to
> the house of the God of Jacob; and he will teach us of his
> ways, and we will walk in his paths: for out of Zion shall
> go forth the law, and the word of Jehovah from Jerusalem.
> And he will judge between the nations, and will decide
> concerning many peoples; and they shall beat their swords
> into plowshares, and their spears into pruning-hooks;
> nation shall not lift up sword against nation, neither shall
> they learn war any more.[5]

All persons get lost at times in a dark world, bogged down in meaninglessness. The state of mind recalls the workers in a factory in Nashville, Tennessee during World War II. They were turning out a peculiarly shaped bit of machinery. What purpose this piece served no one knew. They weren't told, and they weren't supposed to try to find out. Production in that plant lagged until a bright youngster deduced that the article they were producing was a part for an anti-aircraft gun. With that their work took on a new meaning. They were making a weapon that would be used to protect American boys from Japanese and German bombers. The following week they drove pro-duction up twenty-eight percent! How quickly can a flash of meaning, of purposiveness, transform skies that have been little more than a "foul and pestilent congregation of vapours" to a profoundly frustrated Hamlet, into a "majestical roof fretted with golden fire." And when

[5] Isaiah 2.

that golden fire comes, that rubicund brightness coloring the horizons, something we literally see with our eyes, how suddenly our curve of productivity shoots upward!

It was similar for the ancient Jew when he was shown by the prophets that in his sufferings and homelessness there was meaning. Interestingly, the meaning that held for the Jew of ancient times (as it does for Israelite of today) holds also for every other people of the globe. Every people is culturally unique and every people is also a chosen people with a mission. Any nation, however powerful or weak, is participating in and making its own special contribution to the on-going processes of the world revolution that is upon us today. Even the most primitive tribe in the most remote wilderness is contributing to anthropological information something about our own past and the nature of cultures that is invaluable to the understanding of ourselves in these days of change. Thus it is with the United States, with the responsibilities of power thrust upon us by events beyond anyone's designing; our job is to see to the continuance here in America and in the world as a whole of that for which Greece fought and bled at Marathon and Thermopolae and Salamis.

Beyond appearances, however tenebrous, there still is for us, as there was for the ancient Jew, a larger order, a power — call it by what-ever term or name one prefers — a creative destiny in the nature of things. To be effective it must have the cooperation of persons and of peoples who understand that suffering is the price for the realization of that day in a time to come when nation shall no more lift up sword against nation. Once one has made sober covenant with this tendency, shall we call it, in the course of human affairs, and thus has found meaning for some of the sufferings that may well come his way, he is then no longer so homeless in his home or wholly the stranger under the sun.

There will still come hours, as they came to the ancient Jews harried by their own never-ending civil strife and futile rebellions and by the devastations of the invincible legions of Rome, when the promise of a better day seems utterly farfetched, and everything in the world lies in the shadow of a darkness so dark that there is "no brightness in it." It was to this mood of the exile and his defeatist gloom that the rabbis of the talmudic schools of Palestine and Babylonia spoke with their new assurance. "The Temple in Jerusalem may be destroyed," they said in effect. "The Holy City may be lost to us for we know not how long. But for all of these dire calamities and for all of the dreariness of our present surroundings, there is still, back and beyond the strangeness of appearances, the order, the power, the creative destiny in the nature of things, which we call Yahweh. What this order, this power, this destiny is and what it demands of us was supernaturally revealed to the Jews in the Torah, the five books of Moses. If we will but make our lives conform to what is found in the Torah, to what is expected of us by the Power Over All, then will we know whereof the Prophet was speaking when he wrote: 'Holy, Holy, Holy is the Lord of Hosts: the whole earth is full of His glory.' "

With the Torah — which is to say, with the will of God — in his possession, it made no difference how strange and uninviting were the land into which the Jew might wander — Russia, Germany, India, Africa. By studying the Torah and by doing all in his power to dress and eat and drink and regulate his social and family life and talk and think and worship according to its dictates, he established himself, so he believed, in a relationship of warmth and intimacy above that of any other people, with the Head of the household of the world. In the words of Rabbi Louis Finkelstein of the Conservative Jewish Theological Seminary of America: "Judaism is a way of life that endeavors to transform virtually every human action into a means of communion with God."

Bringing virtually every human action into conformity with the will of God as it was found in the Torah was not always a simple matter of "do this, do that — or else." But wherever there was doubt the Rabbis were there and ready with learned interpretations of the Holy Scriptures. Then, as by dialectical necessity, they went on to lengthy interpretations of the earlier interpretations. The result of all this compounding of interpretation was that massive compilation known as the Talmud. The Babylonian Talmud has some 400 sizeable printed pages explaining in detail what is expected of the good Jew in the way of Sabbath observance; some 1,200 equally sizeable pages outlining what is involved in the observance of the several festivals; some 2,000 pages devoted to laws governing the relations of Jew to his fellow men.

It was inevitable that out of the Talmud (with its rabbi interpreters set on transforming every human action into a means of communion with God) should come a distinctive community such as is described

in the recent book of autobiographical writings, *A Village by the Jordan,*
by Joseph Baratz, founder of the Degania colony. Of his boyhood community in the Russian Ukraine he writes:

> *We lived in the Jewish quarter and we were a tradi-*
> *tional community, very different from our Russian neighbors*
> *in looks, manners and customs. The men wore long gab-*
> *ardines and curling side-whiskers; the married women*
> *shaved their heads and put on thick black wigs. Our food*
> *was kosher. Our language was Yiddish . . . Hebrew re-*
> *served for prayers. . . . We had our feasts and our tradi-*
> *tional songs, music and dances. Our schools were the*
> heder *where the usual elementary subjects were taught in*
> Yiddish, *and the* yeshiva, *a Hebrew seminary.*[6]

He writes further that many "distrusted all contacts with the Russians and Russian culture. They said: 'We live in exile, in His own
time He will deliver us and lead us to the Land of Promise; but if we
lose our traditions in the Exile nothing will be left to us.' "

In those distinctive communities the Jew knew a hominess and
coziness, a psychic security that modern man, lost in the anonymity and
vastness of our metropolitan civilization, knows little or nothing of.
How we of this century of the homeless man are to come into the
knowledge of this Jewish kind of community and its sustaining fellowship is one of the most knotty problems of our age. It is imperative,
taking our cue from the traditional Jewish community, that liberal
religious organizations give more heed, far more heed than in the past,
to festival occasions, rituals, even such things as monthly dinners, that
will bring persons more intimately together in fellowship. Then, again,
is it not equally imperative that with these efforts to establish ourselves
more securely in a small circle of fellowship we go on to learn how
to make ourselves at home in the larger social circles of today, for all of
their class exclusion and cultural pluralism and forbidding immensity?

The trend of the times, even in Judaism, is definitely away from
looking for hominess and psychic security only in the isolation of the
distinctive community. Abroad is the conviction that persons must
grow to be big enough to make themselves at home in a vastly larger

[6] Joseph Baratz, *A Village by the Jordan,* (London: The Harvill Press, Ltd.),
p. 2.

national and world-wide universe of discourse. Joseph Baratz complained that the Jews in his home community in the Ukraine were "largely cut off from the outer world; segregated by our own traditions and our fears almost as much as by Russian anti-Semitism we lived timidly in the narrow circle of our small town interests. Many of us felt choked by it." Further good reason for revolt against the talmudic community was expressed some years ago by the Chassidic Jew, Chaim Zhitlowsky. Judaism before the Chassidic revolt of the last century, wrote Zhitlowsky in his preface to *The Dybbuk*,

> *was well on the way to becoming mummified. The study of the Talmud and its innumerable commentaries had absorbed the entire intellectual energies of its men of learning. The greatness of scholars consisted in their ability to unravel Talmudic tangles, rather than in opening new horizons of thought. . . . The religious Jew of that period was like a hypochondriac living in constant terror lest he forget to take this medicine or that at the prescribed moment. A possible omission, "God forbid," of a prayer or ceremony filled him with apprehension.*[7]

Living by way of the commentaries on the Talmud commentaries on the first five books of the Bible — attempting by life-long heroic endeavor at proper eating and dressing and speaking and thinking and praying and festival and Sabbath observances and home rituals, to establish oneself in a relationship of warmth and intimacy with the Head of the household of the world — was foredoomed to failure, unless one had it in him to be satisfied with the limited hominess of the distinctive and all-but-segregated community.

What then is required of one, Jew or Gentile, in this century of the homeless man if, among metropolitan surroundings that leave him lonely and under skies that are not bright, he is to have the vision and the feeling that are comparable to the joyous at-homeness of the Hebrew prophet exulting: "Holy, Holy, Holy is the Lord of Hosts: the whole earth is full of His glory"? To put the question in the language of Jewish scripture: "What doth the Lord require of thee?" The Jew, as has been pointed out, assumed at one time that what

[7] S. Ansky, *The Dybbuk* (Liveright Publishing Corp.), pp. 11-12.

was required of him was the heroic, almost self-immolating effort of living according to the complexities of the talmudic interpretations of Scripture. Earlier, the Jew had imagined that what was required of him was the observance of intricate rituals and much sacrificing in the Temple in Jerusalem. At times, even for centuries on end, he had carried his devotions to the extreme of sacrificing his own first-born child. He was that concerned about squaring himself with the power he believed lay behind appearances, which at times could be so enervatingly dark and glowering.

It was while this sacrificing of first-born children was still a practice that there appeared a prophet of whom increasingly much is being made in Jewish as well as non-Jewish circles. His was a somewhat different answer to the perennial question: "What doth the Lord require?" An example of the person envisioned by the Prophet as coming up to requirement was nicely described by Joseph Baratz.

The man was Aaron David Gordon, already forty-eight years old when he came to Degania, the "kvutza" by the Jordan. He, like Baratz, had emigrated from the Ukraine, where as a youth he refused to let his parents buy him out of Russian military service. It was contrary to his sense of justice that someone else should have to be conscripted in his place. He came to Degania as a well-known socialist writer; but a socialist of the stripe who held that economic reform had to begin with reform of the man. He also believed in and loved manual labor. On his arrival, in the early and rough days of the founding, "nobody believed that he could stand the strain . . . he seemed frail and middle aged . . . like one of those rabbis Rembrandt used to paint." Nevertheless, from earliest morning to dusk he was unfailingly at the side of the other workers, his face streaming with sweat, laboring to exhaustion. But when he tackled any job they noticed that his was work of a different order and quality. Digging ditches for almond trees, for instance, getting so much pay for so many ditches dug, he wasn't among those who scrambled, even quarreled, for more ditches. He proceeded "slowly, calmly, every ditch a masterpiece." Thus was it with all else he did — invariably performing with love, whether sweeping a room or making a bed or plowing in the fields. Such to him, since he "had no fixed dogmatic beliefs," was in large part his religion. He had come to the settlement in sorrow over the recent death of his wife. But after the day's work it was old Gordon who was always to be counted on to talk with anyone who seemed discouraged or depressed; and it was always he who had the energy to lead the singing of the many folk songs he knew so well and to put his whole heart into the dancing. About him Baratz wrote these words:

> *He loved all men, the whole world. He dreamed of a different Palestine, of a different world.*
>
> *He loved children, nature, animals. He was a vegetarian; so were several others of us, but they were not all so kind to their animals. At the midday break, when we were ploughing, some people would leave their mules and hurry off to rest and eat, but Gordon always talked to his mules first and picked grass for them and fed them by hand.*[8]

Little wonder they wrote of him long years after his death: "He was the deepest spiritual influence in our lives."

Here was a man who came about as close as is humanly possible to meeting the requirements of the Prophet Micah: "What doth the Lord require of thee but to do justly, to love mercy, and to walk humbly. . . ." Justly, mercifully, humbly at home with his fellows at Degania and elsewhere in the world he was also, as is invariably the case, wonderfully at home in and happily attuned to the beauty and majesty and mystery, the *glory* of the household of the world in its setting amidst the stars.

[8] J. Baratz, *op. cit.*, pp. 81-82.

Christianity: The Hope of the World?

Put to the professional Christian the question we have asked of each religion in this book, "What do you have for us?" and one will get a reply that most likely will be to this effect: "Application of Christianity to everyday affairs is the only practical hope of the world." That is President Eisenhower. The President's words reflect the new assurance and assertion of contemporary Christianity. This was expressed by Paul Hutchinson of the *Christian Century* in the issue of *Life* devoted to Christianity. Wrote Hutchinson:

> *The churches have a renewed confidence in the relevancy and adequacy of their gospel. This confidence is assuredly not unrelated to the renewed seriousness and respect with which our storm-tossed generation regards the religious approach to life's problems and the Christian explication of its meaning.*

If we of this storm-tossed generation were to take *Life* magazine's special issue on Christianity at its face value, we could expect to find in this religion the final answer to the meaning of life, the ministry to all needs of the spirit. There would be no cause for anyone to be a Jew, Buddhist, Moslem or Vedantist. Christianity would be all things to all men. It would be Judaism offering the sense of at-homeness to all who are homeless in their homes and strangers under the sun. With its cross it would be Buddhism to those who have yet to square themselves with the universality of suffering; Islam to those who would have the strength that comes of the conviction that the tendency toward the good and the right is rooted somehow in the very nature of reality; Vedanta to those who would find their selves. As *the* religion of our American and European culture it is only to be expected that Christianity would do its best to be all things to all men. If it has enjoyed no small success in this endeavor it is hardly to be wondered at, considering all that is included in the rich heritage of this faith.

Included in this heritage is the Jewish heritage, which in itself is a distillation of the religious insights of the Egyptian, Babylonian and Persian civilizations. But included also is the fabulous patrimony of the Greco-Roman pagan world: the Stoicism, the Platonism, the Aristotelianism, the Neo-Platonism, even the Epicureanism, of philosophical and literary Greece, together with rites and festivals and concepts of the many folk and mystery religions of the times. All these many elements, Jewish and pagan, were worked over and unified by the organizing genius of the Romans, and incorporated before the fall of Rome into that amazing composite known as Christianity. Since those days this faith has been the inheritor also of additional cultural riches: the creative and individualistic and dynamic spirit of the Goth; the values of feudalism; and latterly the values of the bourgeois, democratic and industrial revolution.

Christianity, for ought that may be held against it, is truly the cultural Croesus of the religions of the world. Mindful of the extent of this largess of inheritance we now proceed to the more specific question as to what Christianity has specifically for us of this generation. With baptisms, church membership, church attendance and church contributions at an all-time high in America, it would seem that Christianity must have something of inestimable worth for our contemporaries. But exactly what people are getting out of this intensified religiosity is very much of a puzzle. So much of a puzzle is it to churchmen that many are quite forthright in expressing doubts as to its being anything more than a simulant spirituality of positive thinking, a source of emotional "go" for would-be getters, consolation for those made fearful by the unsettlements of automation and the revolution of plenty, as well as by the prospects of atomic and universal war.

Even more of a puzzle — and this brings us to the heart of the problem — is the fact that although Christianity maintains that it is the religion of tenderness and appreciation and brotherly love, it is somehow failing to get through to the heart of modern man. He goes to his church and hears much ado about tenderness and appreciation and the love of one Jesus in whom these values have been raised to the rank of divinity. He knows intuitively that this preaching is spiritually on the right track. But for all of his churchgoing he turns increasingly to such writings as Dr. Smiley Blanton's, *Love or Perish,* or Erich Fromm's latest on love. In his breast, literally in his stomach, he feels the enervating ranklings, the very acid, of his hostilities. He wonders if he ought to try a psychiatrist. He senses that the times, the people he deals with from day to day, his own family, his wife in particular, call for a new kind of person. But what that person is, and how to get to be that person, is the problem that Christianity, with all the respectability, conventionality and dogmatism of its present-day institutional embodiments, seems unable to help him solve.

There was a time when Christianity delivered rather more successfully. In that day men were no less at sea than they are now. They were groping with no less concern toward a new and more adequate kind of being. That time, thanks to what has come from the Dead Sea Scrolls, is more real and meaningful to us than it has been to previous generations. To get there we must go back beyond the days of Paul and the Apostles, beyond Jesus and his Disciples, to certain Jewish fellowships in and about Palestine. We know of these fellowships from the eminent Jewish philosopher, Philo Judaeus of Alexandria, who toured Palestine when Jesus was a child. These groups or colonies he called "Essene." They were non-monastic, and were to be found in and about cities and villages. Their teaching was "piety, holiness, justice, the art of regulating home and city, knowledge of what is really good and bad and of what is indifferent, what ends to avoid, what to pursue — in short, love of God, of virtue, and of man." Philo leaves the impression that they enjoyed a reputation for "kindness," "equality," and "indifference to money."

From Philo we get information that is of greatest significance. But from him we do not get the idea that was the moving inspiration of these brotherhoods. That idea has come to us now at long last from the Dead Sea Scrolls of the Essene monastery at Qumran. From these documents we gather that the members of the various Essene groups were held together by their common desire to assist each other in the cultivation of the holy life that was regarded as the preparation for the coming of the Messiah. The word "Messiah," translated into Greek, is "Christos" or "Christ." Thus to the Greeks and Greek-speaking Jews these Essene groups were known as brotherhoods in the Christ, or Christ brotherhoods. They constituted the pre-Christian Christian church.

If one were to wake up to find himself transported back in time and in the midst of one of the Christ fellowships, he would be amazed at the familiar sound, the Christian ring, of the teachings. In all likelihood he would hear repeated the substance, possibly the actual words, of what is now called the Lord's Prayer. He would be told that, as one of the brotherhood, it was incumbent upon him to love his enemies, to resist not evil, to turn the other cheek, and that "blessed are the meek for they shall inherit the earth." He would be surprised at the striking parallels of the sayings prized by the group with those attributed in the Gospels to Jesus, including the so-called Sermon on the Mount. It is quite probable, moreover, that he would hear not a few of the parables, incorporated later in the New Testament, having to do with the coming and the nature of the new Kingdom of Heaven.

All this is probable from the scholarly and documentary point of view. But it is even more probable because of its being an inevitable consequence of the belief that was the inspiration as well as the central organizing idea of these brotherhoods; the belief that at any hour the Messiah, the Christ, might put in his long-awaited appearance. Coming, no one knew when, but probably soon, was a supernatural deliverer in the form of a man. This being was no mere fantasy to them, but real. He was so real that, as we find in the Qumran documents, they believed that in their services, their sacramental meals, he was already mystically with them and in communion with the brotherhood. To his august side this representative of the Heavenly Father, this perfect person with the power to discern man's every hidden motive, would call the righteous.

Righteousness in those Jewish brotherhoods included, of course, the righteousness of the Ten Commandments and of the Law, and it included the doing justly and loving mercy and humble walking of the prophets. But it included something more that was peculiarly associated with the idea of the coming Messiah, the Christ — a righteousness that was to exceed that of the Scribes and the Pharisees. It came of their idea of the character of the Christ himself. And the idea of his character, as the exemplary character for all men, where did that come from? Not primarily out of revelation. It was made up essentially of everything that out of long experience of man in fellowship with man they had found and knew in their hearts to be finest, most live-with-able, most charming and interesting, most courageous and lovable, most tender and understanding.

What those Jewish brotherhoods hit upon in their concept of the character of the Christ was vastly more than any of them ever knew.

It was more than the Christian Church (into which they presently evolved) ever grasped except in occasional flashes. It was, in a word, one of the essentials of all civilized religion, a kind of universal Christ. This ideal made its appearance, beginning about 600 B.C., in all the leading religions of the world. Every one of the founders of the world's religions, including Mohammed, was transformed by his followers into a Christ-like being. The universality of the Christ ideal is illustrated in the several scriptures of the religions. Each has its version of the concept, for example, of returning good for evil. Let the reader pick, if he can, which of the following is Christian:

1. "Let a man overcome wrath by calmness, evil by good. Let him subdue the miser by liberality, the liar by truth."
2. "Your good, and that alone, I seek.
   Howe'er your anger you may wreak."
3. "Wound not another, though by him provoked. Do no one injury by thought or deed. Utter no word to pain thy fellow-creatures."
4. "Overcome evil with good. Turn aside evil with that which is better."
5. "Recompense injury with kindness."
6. "If thine enemy be hungry, give him bread to eat. And if he be thirsty, give him water to drink."
7. "But love ye your enemies. And do good. And lend, hoping for nothing again." [1]

This Christ idea or ideal (or shall we say spirit?) was no mere lifeless ethical abstraction. What it meant, where it meant anything at all, was the strength, the renewal of life, the new man, such as the people of India found in Gandhi. He more than any other person of our times was the exemplar of the spirit of "inasmuch as ye have done it unto the least of these ye have done it unto me." Where as few as two or three are gathered in the spirit of the Christ there the mind of each is free to let go and give of itself in all honesty and without fear. The feeling state of one enhances that of his friend. Then with mind supplementing mind, the totality of one's life experience supplementing

[1] Robert E. Hume, *Treasure House of the Living Religions* (Charles Scribner's Sons), pp. 224-229. The sources, in their order, are: Buddhist; Confucianist; Hindu; Moslem; Taoist; Jewish; Christian.

that of another, heart enlarged by heart, the group generates out of itself a larger mind and larger heart. Of all possible communions with the more-than-self there is none more inspiring, enriching, and elevating. One does not wonder at Christians explaining this experience as a personal visitation of the divine Christ.

Perhaps we had better remind ourselves at this juncture that we are not discussing Jesus; only the Christ idea and ideal or spirit and its power. In the historic Jesus were traits that towards the end of his life put some few of those who knew him best in mind of the Christ. But there was also in the man Jesus enough of class hatred, enough of the spirit of bringing the sword and not peace, enough of regard for a flaming hell of eternal punishment, enough of bitterness and contempt (denouncing those he disliked as snakes and sons of snakes) to raise grave questions as to the feasibility of his identification with the Christ. Relegating Jesus to the background and playing up only such of his sayings and lineaments of character as fitted into the universal Christ ideal, emphasizing withal the theology of his death and resurrection, was no oversight or act of stupidity on the part of Christian theologians.

One in whom his fellow men discerned the Christ character, the spirit of the Christ ideal, was the New Jersey Quaker, John Woolman. Sailing to England he refused the luxury of a ship's cabin and put up, instead, in the steerage, "in order to share with the sailors the experience of the worst possible quarters." In England he held that inasmuch as coach horses were being whipped literally to their deaths, and inasmuch as the English let coach boys be exposed in the open to the point of freezing to death, they were doing all this to him. So in good conscience he could do no more than walk. And walk he did, the length of England!

A true exemplar of the Christ spirit, Woolman didn't go about condemning anyone, throwing stones at the sinner, making people wretched with guilt. The genuinely Christ-like person never does that sort of thing. When with him one doesn't feel like a no-good or an ignoramus. One doesn't feel like an inferior. So disarmingly simple, common and even commonplace is he, that in his company one is more free, more his intellectual and social best self — as people discovered when John Woolman was their guest.

He was once invited to the farm home of Thomas Woodard, of London Grove, Pennsylvania. That was in the middle 1700's. It was the occasion of a quarterly meeting of the Friends. When the time arrived for serving the dinner he was not among the guests. He had been there earlier. A search revealed that his hat and his horse also were missing. Tom Woodard and his wife exchanged knowing glances. Woolman, they surmised, had seen their one slave, old Bet, busying herself with the preparations. To have remained for dinner would have meant his being the recipient of a service that was forbidden to one who would also carry with him in his heart the spirit of the Christ. Tom Woodard, after a sleepless night, turned to his wife at his side: "My dear, we will have to free Bet." Mrs. Woodard broke down and wept. But later that morning the three went to the justice's office to sign the papers of manumission — for as Mr. and Mrs. Woodard both agreed, they could not afford to keep old Bet a slave if it meant barring John Woolman from their parlor and table. Thanks to the beautifully persuasive example of Woolman and others of his spirit, there was by 1788 "not a single Quaker-owned slave on the American continent."

John Woolman would have been much taken with those early Essene brotherhoods in Christ. He would have been struck by the similarity of their communism with the communistic community of Apostolic Christians described in the Book of Acts. He would have noted the common storehouse of provisions, the common store of clothes, the common treasury, the warmth of fellowship. All this has been characteristic for many years of the Jewish colony, Degania, the village by the Jordan alluded to in the chapter on Judaism. As a result of their one-for-all, all-for-one devotion to the common cause, the Essenes, like the Jews of Degania, doubtless worked and played with prodigious energy and endurance. There was an intimacy and depth and a richness of fellowship such as probably only the Jew can know. John Woolman would have approved and he would have been reasonably at home, except for one obstacle, one unavoidable obstacle — felt by the members of the community as well as by a Woolman.

It was when that obstacle was surmounted that these groups ceased to be Jewish as such and became Christian. It came about in this wise: one of the brotherhood, face livid with excitement, panting from his running, rushed in one day from Jerusalem. What he managed to pour out was to this effect: "You remember that man Jesus, follower of our brother, John the baptizer? The Jesus who we heard was carrying on with John's preaching of the coming of the Kingdom? The Jesus who was so successful as a faith healer that crowds sprang up about him and followed him wherever he went? Well, he was in Jerusalem during the Passover, and things got out of hand. Afraid of what the crowds might be up to, Pontius Pilate ordered him seized, crucified — and then — then — and, believe me, I have talked with those who swear they saw him — after three days he rose from the dead! That man Jesus was the Christ! He has proved it by rising from the dead! In no time at all he'll be back, appearing among the clouds and shining in all the glory of the Christ!" Exactly what happened on that occasion we will probably never know. But that numbers of people were convinced there were post-mortem appearances of one sort or another is beyond question.

With the Christ's coming so near at hand, with emphasis on tenderness, on appreciation of each other, on love, encumbent upon them now as never before, what about the Gentile? What about the Syrian neighbor next door, the Greek and the Roman neighbor? Of the Gentile neighbor a Brother could honestly say that inasmuch as anything was done to him it was done to the Brother. He was worthy of every possible consideration, including justice and kindness and, if need be, the cloak off the back of the Brother. He was to have all these things, with but one reservation. He was to remember that the fellowship of this Jewish brotherhood was too precious, too sacred, to permit their throwing open wide the gates of membership to all peoples of all nations.

But the Christ, was he to be the Christ only of the Jew? Was the brotherhood of the new Kingdom of Heaven to be the brotherhood of the Jew exclusively? If one were to be the exemplar of the spirit of "inasmuch as ye have done it unto the least of these," could he avoid being the exemplar also of the kindred and inseparable spirit of "come unto me all ye that labor and are heavy laden"? Come unto me, yes, into our midst, into the brotherhood which has meant life and life more abundant to all of us. The moment the Jew opened wide the arms of his precious fellowship, something astounding happened to him. With the leveling of all barriers between man and man, with his inmost being reunited to humanity and unified, he was seized by, convulsed by, an uprush of long-repressed emotion that had him literally beside himself, shouting, jabbering, weeping, prophesying. This is the ever recurring picture in Apostolic literature of what was explained as the seizure of the Holy Spirit.

As the act of embracing men and women and children of all nations transformed Paul, the ineffectual, and hundreds of fellow Jews into flaming evangelists to be stopped by nothing, neither fire nor sword nor scorn, the same act of inclusion also worked prodigies of transformation in the Gentile. So illuminating to the Gentile was the new profundity of meaning, and so rejuvenating the experience, that Christian brotherhoods rose up and spread as if by miracle. Commenting on the causes for the success of Christianity, the late Gilbert Murray, an eminent classical scholar, wrote in a somewhat similar vein:

> *When I try to realize it as a sort of semi-secret society for mutual help with a mystical religious basis, resting first on the proletariates of Antioch and the great commercial manufacturing towns of the Levant, then spreading by instinctive sympathy to similar classes in Rome and the West . . . the various historical puzzles begin to fall into place. Among other things this explains the strange subterranean power by which the Emperor Diocletian was baffled, and to which the pretender Constantine had to capitulate; it explains its humanity, its intense feeling of brotherhood within its own bounds, its incessant care for the poor. . . .[2]*

Wherever Christianity breathes the spirit of open-armed inclusiveness — inclusiveness apart from the exclusiveness of respectability, apart from the exclusiveness of conventionality and apart from the exclusiveness of dogmatism — there Christianity delivers. It ministers to the times. It is a ministry, let there be no mistaking about it, that is no monopoly of those who can repeat, "I believe in God the Father Almighty, Maker of heaven and earth: And in Jesus Christ His only Son our Lord . . ." As inclusive brotherhood it is the religion of all good men, holy and catholic. The Christ spirit, which in one sense is with us as a larger group-mind and heart when we are gathered together at our finest and best, and yet in another sense is ever the anticipated one, may well be "the only practical hope of the world."

Certain it is that our war-plagued generation can look nowhere else with greater profit and hope. Violate the Christ spirit (as did the French with their inscription on the monument erected on the spot of

[2] Gilbert Murray, *Five Stages of Greek Religion* (Columbia University Press), p. 233.

the signing of the armistice of the First World War — "Here succumbed the criminal pride of the German Empire") and nations go on from war to war without end. Equal to the criminal pride of the German Empire was the criminal pride of the French. The attitude of Christian nation toward so-called Christian nation has in it still too much of the anti-Christ spirit of the nurse in Homer's *Odyssey*. After Odysseus returns to his beloved Ithaca and slaughters the despicable suitors, the nurse exclaims gleefully to Penelope: "It would have warmed your heart to see Odysseus, like a lion, dabbled with blood and gore." In a world of her kind, pride will go on begetting hate. Our only real hope, as in Homeric times, is in the answering caution of good Penelope: "Dear nurse, be not too . . . filled with glee." Previously Odysseus had cautioned: "Old woman, rejoice in silence; restrain yourself, and do not make any noise about it; it is an unholy thing to vaunt over dead men." Something terrible has happened, Penelope and her husband are saying in effect, and we would fall short of our human stature and dignity if we failed to recognize the horror of it. Penelope, speaking as she did for the Christ spirit, might well caution us: "Be not too boastful America, or filled with glee at every sign of trouble for the colossus beyond the sea."

The spirit we invoke has ever been associated in men's minds with the miraculous. Carried to skid row and speaking with words of love to the unlovable down-and-outer it does come, as it did with Sam Hadley of a generation ago, as a wonder-working power. Hadley was pleading one night with his usual floater audience. If only they would let Christ come into their hearts! He was interrupted by a physician who had wandered out of sheer curiosity into the Hadley Mission. "Mr. Hadley, you have been appealing here with a glowing passion to these drunkards for a new and made-over life. I speak as a physician to say that you would not talk to these men thus if you had ever seen what the inside of a drunkard's stomach looks like." Without a split second's hesitation Hadley shot back: "Sir, I had a drunkard's stomach and Jesus Christ saved me from it, and saves me from it now." With that Christ spirit in the heart there is healing for the injured flesh and there is less occasion for the drunkenness that so regularly is a symptom of failure to reach wife and fellowmen.

Too often people associate the word "Christian" only with the spectacular: the martyr, the saint, the missionary, the celibate — and even the Holts of Cresswell, Oregon, who adopted, in addition to their own six children, eight Korean war orphans. It has long seemed to me that the great spirit we have been considering would be incredibly more sustaining and meaningful if it were invoked more often in out-of-the-way places where there is no glory, such as in the little restaurant I stopped at a few years ago in Kansas City.

The restaurant was new. I was there just after one o'clock. The noon rush was over. The owner was chatting from behind the counter with a customer. "I had a real Christian in here yesterday," he said. "Yessiree, a real Christian." He went on. "It was this a'way. It was a woman. She was seated at the counter and just as her plate was shoved up to her, down that counter in front paraded five cockroaches; a big one and four little ones, all in a line. Where those blankety blank things came from is beyond me. But there she sat staring at them filthy things. What was she going to do? The place was full. Was she going to kick up a row and put a crab on my business? I saw her hesitate, open her mouth, look disgusted. Boy was I scared! Then she pulled her face together. She smiled. 'Gosh!' she said good and loud and making people laugh. 'Them cockroaches sure is sociable!' " The restaurant proprietor was right. In that moment his patron was a Christian.

The sum of these many little daily encounters where there is neither recognition nor glory comes close to making up the total of life for all of us. It is in these encounters in the obscurity of home and out-of-the-way places where the invoking of the Christ spirit spells not only more abundant life but also, possibly, the "only practical hope of the world."

Ethical Religion: A New World Religion?

The message of this concluding chapter is a call to all religious liberals: "Let's have an end to apologizing for being liberal, for being small in number and inconsequential, for being pariahs in a world of religious conformity. The hour is at hand for us to lift up our heads. Ours, if only because we are liberal and open, is the heritage, as we have been trying to bring out in these chapters, of whatever there is of value in the world's great religions. But more than this, we can lift up our heads because we belong to something that is greater than we know. Together, in what our various liberal communions hold in common, in the meeting of present-day human needs of the spirit to which we alone can minister, we constitute another distinct family among the world's great religions."

One should point out, and this merely by way of introduction, that these several liberal religious persuasions minister, as can none of the conventionally religious groups, not merely to the needs of thinking men for intellectual honesty in religion, but also, and more importantly, to those further and more pressing needs that inevitably arise, as the consequence of the insistence upon honesty in religion. When myth — myth of creation, myth of virgin birth, resurrection, revelation, heaven, hell, talmudic law — gives way to mystery, there liberal religion is ready and at hand to minister with that which, while accepting mystery, turns it into majesty and gives one a sense of social belonging and at-homeness in the universe. The emphasis of this ministry is on the ethical rather than the theological; on reverence for life rather than dogmatic correctness; on concern for the heaven that lies about us when we are evoking the best in each other, rather than for some heaven in the hereafter. This ethical orientation is nowhere better symbolized than in the scene that is so much the favorite of Chinese art, the three laughing philosophers. One was a Buddhist abbot, the second a Confucian scholar, the third a Taoist sage. These old men had met for the day at the Buddhist monastery. On leave-taking the three walked side by side down the path. So engrossing was the conversation that the abbot, without being aware of it, walked across the bridge which, according to a vow he had taken, he was never to cross. Suddenly he awakened to what he had done. He threw up his hands in dismay. Then, instead of groaning with fear or guilt, the abbot burst out with the other two in gales of merry laughter. More to be revered than a superstitious vow or the letter of the law is the understanding and tolerant human being with a sense of humor.

That the various liberal religious groups, taken in their wholeness, constitute another family of the world's great religions is realized only when we pass beyond introductory characterizations to the larger perspective in which we see these groups in revolt against inadequate and outmoded concepts and practices of the traditional faiths. All the members of this liberal family of religions are in revolt, whether they are conscious of it or not, against the degrading, guilt-evoking, unnatural standards and ideals of those who, having made a profession or a vocation of conventional religion, insist that they are the shining examples of spiritual achievement; that theirs is the only way to salvation and peace with God and man. Powering the revolt is the profound distress of spirit of the man and woman who are engrossed in the breath-taking task of raising a family; who labor in the home to make it a smooth-working, attractive, comfortable and cozy refuge; who strive in their occupations to get somewhere, to contribute something, to amount to something; who try to do their parts as responsible citizens in the schools, in the government, in social welfare. But despite their well-meaning efforts, and the maturity of character that may come of their efforts, and despite the blessing they may be each to the other, their children and their friends, these persons find themselves classified by the professionally religious as creatures of a lower level of spirituality. They live, they are told, on a lower plane of spiritual development. High above them, surrounded by a carefully nurtured aura of reverence, are those who have renounced marriage and home and job and earthly reward, and who have made of religion a full-time vocation. In this aura of reverence move, also, many a Protestant clergyman and bearded rabbi, who have also renounced the worldly to the extent of elevating themselves to a realm somewhat above the sordidly secular.

Those who make of orthodox religion a full-time vocation never tire of pointing out that home and getting ahead on the job and devotion to the P.T.A. are secular and are not enough. Such was the recent sermon of a Lutheran professor of theology over a St. Louis radio station. No one's life is complete, he affirmed over and again, until he has surrendered to the example of Jesus. In everything Jesus did he was wholly dependent upon God and in the service of God. In his praying he served God. In his healing of the lame and the blind he served God. In his calling of the Disciples and his teaching he served God. In the many activities that culminated in his crucifixion he served God. All in all, his was a life whose full-time vocation was religious. Similarly, it is only to the extent that the layman can fit everything he does into a context of prayer, Bible reading, worship, charity, self-sacrifice, abstention and zeal in converting others that he even begins to approach perfection, and his vocation becomes acceptable in the sight of God.

The professor is only the Christian counterpart of what we find in all the world's great religions: those who make a vocation of their religion, who set themselves up as the ideal for all men, and their practice as the standard for all walks of life. One runs into this in early Judaism in the urge of the rabbis to transform all Israel into a nation of priests. It is much the same again in Islam and Vedanta, and especially so in Buddhism. The person who goes into any one of these religions to make of it his full-time vocation is compelled to find in it the psychological counterpart of what therapy the average man and woman get from the striving and the problem-solving of home and job and community effort. As the average man and woman derive the better part of their personality integration from their secular involvements, so the one who makes a profession of religion must find a comparable integration of personality in his religious involvements. If, for instance, the goal of the professional is moral perfection and saintliness, he must work at mortifying the flesh, fasting, praying, meditating on his sins and converting others. If his mind is to be integrated into the totality of his personality it must be occupied continuously with knotty theological problems, with scriptural learning, and the subtleties of philosophy and moral science. If his emotions are to be integrated along with his mind, he must perform the numerous devotions that will put him into a loving mood toward God and brothers. And then, if his very muscles and energies are to be integrated, as they must be, they will have to be exercised in the numerous day and night marches to chapel, the genuflexions of the devotions, the chores of the establishment, and then in the quieting of the muscles in mystic concentration.

The religious professional is driven more by psychological necessity than by anything purely spiritual. He has no choice but to find in the practices of traditional religion the occupation for the mind, the outlets for the emotions, the activities for muscles crying for employment, the goals of striving, that will bring all the many elements of selfhood into a focus of integration. As a consequence, the professional makes of religion and the religious life a fantastically complicated maze of theological subtlety, devotional sentimentality and moral picayunishness. With little else but the intricacies of their faith to occupy their thoughts, monkish minds pile commentary on commentary. They turn the verses of a Sermon on the Mount into as many books. They subdivide an eightfold path into eighty paths, and then multiply the sum. They listen to the Buddhist brother reciting scripture — each sentence a subject for hours, even months, of meditation and practice:

> *If the brahmana [a monk of the highest achievement] has reached the other shore in both insight, in restraint and contemplation, all bonds vanish from him who has obtained knowledge. . . .*
>
> *I do not call a man a brahmana because of his origin or of his mother. He is indeed arrogant, and he is wealthy: but the poor who is free from all attachments, him I call indeed a brahmana.*
>
> *Him I call indeed a brahmana who, after cutting all fetters, never trembles, is free from bonds and unshackled.*
>
> *Him I call indeed a brahmana who, after cutting the strap and the thong, the rope with all that pertains to it, has destroyed all obstacles and is awakened.*
>
> *Him I call indeed a brahmana who, though he has committed no offense, endures reproach, stripes, and bonds; who has endurance as his force and strength for his army. . . .*[1]

And so proceeds the reading, "Him I call indeed a brahmana who," on and on, with dozens of these characterizations.

Those who make a vocation of religion transform it, as they have

---

[1] F. Max Müller, *Sacred Books of the East* (Charles Scribner's Sons), XII, 92-93.

transformed the major portion of each of the world's religions, into something that for the most part is radically different from what is needed by today's man and woman, whose vocation, and hence whose integration, is largely the more normal and natural life of breadwinning and homemaking. Little wonder that increasing numbers of men and women are in revolt. Theirs is a demand for religion that is pre-eminently a religion of, by and for laymen. They insist in unequivocal language: "Our vocation is one for which we do not have to apologize! Living our lives as nature intended, as husband and wife, raising children and doing the work of the world is man's true calling and his natural vocation. We are not going to let any professional Christian or professional Jew, or Buddhist or Moslem for that matter, weigh us down with the guilty feeling that his calling is morally superior and of the divine, while ours is but a compromise with animal instincts, with human weaknesses and with the devil. If any vocation is to be regarded as good and as sacred, ours is that vocation!"

In their devotion to the work of the world, American laymen have accomplished one thing that all the prayers and sacrifices and ascetic lives of the professionals were unable to effect. They conquered the economic scarcity which for thousands of years has been the main concern of man and the burden of his prayers. This conquest is one of the great landmarks of human achievement. In conquering scarcity men also cut away the ground from under the old spirituality of scarcity that went hand in hand with economic want. And so today, as a consequence of doing away with scarcity and the necessity for its accompanying spirituality, Americans are beginning to find themselves derelicts and all but foundering in a veritable sea of abundance. To make the most of this abundance and give it some kind of meaning they must have, they are discovering, a new vision; in so many words, a new spirituality of abundance. They know they need this new spirituality because they know, out of the depths of personal unrest, that intensified devotion to the work of the world is not enough; also in addition, that marriage and home and P.T.A. activities are not enough to bring to a radiantly healthy focus the many wondrous elements of the human psyche. All of this brings to mind again what we touched on earlier in connection with the idea of the place of ethical religion among the world religions: the liberals' outgrowing of the ancient spirituality of scarcity and with it their quest for a spirituality of health and plenty, establishes the family of liberal religion even more securely and uniquely as one among the world's great faiths.

The urgency of this quest for a spirituality of plenty speaks convincingly from a letter received some months ago by someone who specializes in giving advice to troubled adults. The letter writer states that he is sixty, his wife, forty-six; that they are living on "an income of $510.00 a month in one of the retirement paradises." Plenty of food, plenty of clothes, plenty in the way of housing, plenty of time for recreation, plenty in cultural opportunities. How happy they should be! The plenty they enjoy is in ever-increasing measure the good fortune of the bulk of Americans. Soon everybody, retired or not, is to have this plenty and this leisure. But for the retired pair, as for everyone else who has yet to learn how to make the most of the abundance that is the realization of the dream of the ages, there is something lacking. The writer of the letter has been advised by his doctor to "find some work." Why work? After a business career that has taken him over the world for twenty-five years, he has to say about his retirement paradise, "We find it uninteresting . . ." To find such an existence uninteresting is to find it disintegrating to the personality.

For this pathetic state of mind there is no real help to be had from the spirituality of scarcity. Its ministry was for the man who, like so many millions of Hindus and Chinese today, was hungry much of the time. Along with that hunger he also suffered from a distress that was even more painful than the debilitating gnawing of his stomach. The hunger pangs reminded him that he was a nobody in a society in which being sleek and well fed symbolized the somebody. To this hungry nobody the spirituality of scarcity came in the ministering person of one who had responded to the admonition to "sell all thou hast" and join the ranks of the poor. The rich, according to his outlook, had no more chance to get into heaven than had a camel to get through the eye of a needle. Joining the ranks of the poor, the religious professional went on to make a virtue of hunger, calling it fasting. He made it a deliberate mortification of the flesh and, as such, an offering of the body as a living sacrifice to the Lord. In making a virtue of what was a near-universal necessity among the bulk of his fellow men the religious professional became a somebody in the sight of God. In his company the poor man began to see himself also as a somebody in the sight of God. So it was with scarcities of clothes and fuel and shelter. Here again, the hero, the "athlete" of the spirituality of scarcity, with his bare and unheated cell, his bench bed, his rough-woven, fashionless and comfortless garb, shone as the light of the spirit. And for countless men and women who were forever wrestling with those reputedly unspiritual impulses that meant bringing more babies into homes where there was no food and no room for more babies, there was still the shining example of the religious professional, his celibacy and his sacrifices. For these austerities and privations the rewards in the life to come were to be rich beyond all imagining.

But in all this — unhappily still the basic pattern of what passes for spirituality in our culture — what is there for the couple on $510 a month in a retirement paradise? What for any and all the rest of us, blessed as we are with an ever-increasing abundance? Sell all we have and send the proceeds to Africa or India? Go there ourselves? What about the remaining millions of Americans whose spiritual problem is even more acute than it is for those who, although they may be suffering from want, have still the spirituality of scarcity to which they can look for consolation and self-respect? The adult advisor suggested to the letter writer that he might set up a small private business on which he and his wife could focus their attention and surplus energies. In other words, get back to work. But work for what? For the sake of piling up more money for a more expensive paradise? For the compulsive sake of work itself? Keeping busy?

The answer to such questions, wrote John Knox Jessup of *Life* magazine in the issue devoted to Christianity, is to be found in Christianity. He stated that in this religion is the wherewithal to make work meaningful, to make it "consecrated." He went on to say (falling back, incidentally, on the concept that is the key concept of the spirituality of scarcity), that the meaning resides in the heavenly "world that lies beyond this world." Thus, for some strange reason that has never been satisfactorily explained, the souls of the starved and the deprived and the sad and the bored are somehow going to be happy forever, doing nothing but being happy in the retirement paradise of the universe!

Exactly what constitutes a spirituality for an age of plenty has yet to be worked out. But for this job there is no group that is better fitted than the men and women of the liberal, which is to say ethical, faiths who insist, to begin with, that man's number one job, his sacred and basic vocation, is living his life as nature intended he should, with a woman, raising children, devotedly doing the work of the world. All this is not enough, as we have observed. A truly adequate vocation for the whole of man demands additional interests, additional ideals and dreams, worlds beyond worlds for his adventuring. And so it is that ethical religion looks beyond the ancient scriptures of the religions of scarcity to the new vistas, the truly new universe now being opened to us by the many spectacular advances in psychiatry; to the new heavens of astronomy and earth satellites and the possibilities of space travel; to the ever-alluring realms of possibility revealed by genius expressing itself in music and poetry and fiction and the colorful imaginings of the artists; to the release that belongs to those who are learning to live in open-armed brotherhood with the peoples of all nations and all races.

Prominent among the spiritual pioneers of our new age will be no sanctimonious monks and nuns or starveling preachers; no professional advertising by his conspicuous garb and his prowess in self-denying selflessness and world-denying other-worldliness. Self-denial in the interest of richer interrelationships there will be, of course. And detachment from the overwhelming plenitude of things there will also have to be. But the new spirituality will partake far more of the combined detachment and appreciation of Henry David Thoreau. One afternoon he was eyed from a distance by an unfriendly farmer. The countryman's manner and posture radiated the threatening suspicion that Thoreau had stolen apples from his orchard. Actually, said Thoreau, what he was taking away with him was not a paltry few apples but the better part of the man's farm. It is this, the spirituality that gives to every other thing its value, whether it be a crust of bread or an income of $510.00 a month in a retirement paradise, that is probably the main concern today of ethical religion. And prominent in these circles is not the lone ascetic but rather the family in whose wise use of plenty others discern an exemplary flowering of flesh and mind and heart and spirit.

Not overlooked in this quest for a more adequate spirituality are the facts of pain and frustration and death. Ethical religion, generically speaking, is anything but the fair weather faith of superficial optimism it has been painted to be by its conventionally religious detractors. Ethical Culture, for instance, has always been very much alive to the tragic. Early in his ministry in New York City, Ethical Culture's founder,

Felix Adler, was overwhelmed time and again by the omnipresence of suffering: man's inhumanity to man, uncalled-for disease, inexcusable poverty, human beings degraded to grubbing and a mere animal subsistence. These facts he did not evade or try to explain away with neat theological or philosophical formulas. They were facts he had to live with, in the persons to whom it was his duty to minister.

It is here again, in the meeting of misfortune and suffering, that the family of liberal religion stands out distinctively as a great new religion among the religions of the world. For men and women of the liberal following the grim facts of pain and death are not to be erased by assurances to the effect that presently, in some hereafter of bliss, there will be never another hurt or parting. That there may be such a hereafter is by no means beyond the realm of possibility. But what may be possible is not to be taken by liberals as a pretext for dodging the reality of death and its shattering impact in the here and the now. For these liberals there is no escape in calling upon the supernatural for interference to save a loved one from incurable cancer or muscular dystrophy, or to restore one's lost fortune or good name, or to send a Messiah to smite the Hitler or the Stalin. There is hope, always, in human effort; but meanwhile, until human effort conquers this evil or that, there is ever the immediate fact of miscalculation, mischance, or calamity.

Felix Adler wrote about pain; how it builds about us a high wall that shuts us in on ourselves and makes us prisoners. Pain, he went on, can lay one low. It can leave one "almost too weak to raise a finger." But even at that low ebb a person need not be downed to the point where the self lets things *get* the self, where one is moody or complaining and feels sorry for himself. In that abject state the self is submerged. There is then no giving of the self. And when there is no giving of self to others, the ultimate in deprivation results: the utter loss and finally the despair that is the lot of anyone who has to live or work with one who is habitually withdrawn and submerged in his troubles. However, as Adler pointed out, we do have it in our power, no matter what the circumstances, to say through the expression of the eye, through the tone of the voice, however feeble, that here is someone, a self, that can rise above self-concern and consider the problems of those who wait on him. He can exercise a certain kind of strength of spirit which, as Adler put it, "no one can resist."

That Adler gave voice to reality I can attest to, with a conviction born of more than a quarter of a century of ministering to liberal men and women as they met death, or lost precious children, or were robbed, during the depression, of everything they possessed. Seldom have I left the presence of a victim of calamity or a stricken one with a feeling of anything but inspiration or outright elation. Typical of their spirit was the response of a grand old pillar of my Evanston congregation. At seventy-four he had lost everything in a financial crash. Two years later he passed out cards announcing his new business address. He was only nicely under way in this new venture when some valuable but non-negotiable securities, belonging to a client, were stolen from his side at a bank teller's window. At the same time came another blow that would have crushed any man of lesser stature; a physical ailment that demanded an immediate and serious major operation. On taking my leave of the elderly patient in the hospital, shortly before the operation, I failed, I am afraid, to convey in the tone of my voice the reassurance that should have been there. I said: "Well, we'll be seeing you." Instantly the answering voice rang out strong and clear: "I'll be back." His affirmation was not mere swagger. It was the response of one who would permit nothing to get him down. He did come back, as courageous persons so regularly do. They do come back and they keep on coming when their spirits are up, rather than down, and when their spirits are going out in a manner that "no one can resist." It is from these stricken ones, who may seem to themselves to have the least to offer, that the strong and the healthy and the hopeful get part of the lift that carries them over the roughest places and gives them the inspiration to keep on going.

Some 1900 years ago, at a spot called Golgotha, near Jerusalem, there hung, nailed to a cross, a would-be savior of the Jewish nation; a most dismal end for what, according to New Testament records, must have been at its outset a promising career as a healer, a speaker; a magnetic leader of men, a national hero. Certain in his own mind that the time for God's long-awaited supernatural intervention was at hand, he had arranged for a triumphal entry into Jerusalem; he had boldly defied the religious and civil authorities and cleansed the temple of its money-changers. But then nothing happened — no earthquake, no darkening of the sun, no rushing of mighty winds, but instead he was seized, condemned, scourged, and ignominiously nailed to the cross.

Alone, in physical agony, betrayed by one disciple, denied by his favorite, abandoned by the rest, howled down by the mob, what was this but the absolute triumph of circumstance? Finally came the dismal wail of inner defeat, to be found in both Matthew and Mark, and probably authentic: "My God, my God why hast thou forsaken me?"

In the Gospel of Luke we find somewhat different words put into the mouth of the defeated and dying savior. Luke is known as the Greek gospel. It is this Greek influence we see reflected in the only words the author of this book could conceive as befitting the last utterance of one who was supposed to represent humanity at its best. The author expresses, in his idea of fitting last words, the spiritual maturity of the Greek tragedies in which the beholder saw the hero going down under the bludgeonings of inexorable circumstance to defeat and death — going down outwardly, but not inwardly. Witnessing those elevating dramatic spectacles, portraying as they did men who were at their best when times were at their worst, the mature beholder found inspiration to carry on against adversity with courage and nobility. What the writer of the Gospel of Luke puts into the mouth of the dying hero are words, not of wretched despair, not of hate, not of condemnation for those who had triumphed over him, but rather: "Father, forgive them for they know not what they do."

Luke is most admirable in his insistence that if one who supposedly was the hero, the divine-like person, didn't actually rise above despair on the cross and utter these words, he should have. In this Luke speaks not for revelation and not for historic fact but for the spirit of man at its best. With this exalted sentiment, the story of the Christ might well have found its fitting conclusion. It stands in no need of the Hollywood-like supplement of Resurrection and Ascension and triumphal Second Coming; of the supernatural intervention that turned defeat into something that wasn't really external defeat, death into a state that was not death after all. "Father, forgive them for they know not what they do" are words, not of a God triumphant, but of the universal human spirit towering undefeated above circumstance.

Index

Adler, Dr. Felix, 102, 103, 104
Agni, 27
Ali, Ameer, 37, 39
Amos, 75
Analects: effect on China, 13; inadequacy of translation, 14
Aristophanes, 69
Arjuna, 27
Asceticism, 41
Ascetics: Hindu, 8; Christian, 102
Atman, 33

Baratz, Joseph, 80, 81, 82, 83
Benton, Thomas H., 30-31
Bhagavad Gita, 27, 29
Bodhi tree, 4, 5, 9, 10
Buber, Martin, 73
Buddha, 7, 9, 62, 63
Buddhism: a family of religions, 1-3; Hinayana, 2; Theravada, 2; Mahayana, 2; and suffering, 5-8; and grief, 9-10; as professionalism, 97
Buddhist: philosophy, 1; heaven, 2; self-centeredness, 2; complexity, 3; prayer, 3; humanism, 3; serenity, 4; monasteries, 4; enlightenment, 4, 9, 10; eight-fold path, 8-9; brahmana, 98
Byrnes, Justice James, 21

Chale: Moslem convert, 43, 44
Chi K'ang, 16
Chuangtse, 54-55
Christ: and Buddha, 63; brotherhoods, 86; spirit of, 88, 89, 91, 92, 93; as divine, 89; as healer, 93; crucified, 104-105
Christian: orthodox, 11; absurdities, 35; puritanism, 41; professional, 84, 99; resurgence, 85; respectability, 85; teachings, 87; apostolic, 91; inclusiveness, 92
Christian Century, 84

Christianity: in Spain, 37; and women, 41; and success, 92; hope of the world, 84, 93; in *Life*, 101
Christians: versus Moslems, 37
Chrysostom, 41
Cobb, Irving, 30
Communion: nature, 47-50, 52; talmudic, 79; Christian, 88-89
Communist principles, 15
Community: Jewish, 80
Confucian: way, 21; gentleman, 19, 20-21; versus Taoists, 50, 51; politeness, 21; scholars, 56, 62
Confucius: peculiarities, 12-13; and women, 12; on music, 12-13; on himself, 13, 21-22; not conservative, 13; times of, 14; defiance of Chi K'ang, 16; message to his times, 16; student disciples of, 17; wanderings of, 17; isolated, 19; and ambitions of students, 20; teaching, 50
Contemplative: Taoist, 47-48
Courage, 31, 29-30, 104
Creel, Dr. H. G., 13, 16, 21

Dante: on Mohammed, 38
Dead Sea Scrolls, 86
Degania, 80, 83, 90
Desire: as suffering, 7; control of, 8
Disciples: of Confucius, 17; of Jesus, 86
Douglas, Justice William O., 34, 36, 42, 44

Ecclesiastes, 64-65
Eisenhower, President, 84
Emerson: on the oversoul, 33
Empathy, 32
Enlightenment: Buddhist, 4, 9, 10; Zen, 62, 63, 67, 70
Epicureanism, 85
Essenes, 86, 90
Ethical Culture, 102

107